DR. FOUNT SHULTS

T-SHIRTS
& OVERCOATS

Who
Am I
Really?

T-shirts and Overcoats:
Who am I really …
underneath my cover?

Fount Shults

First edition published May 2016

ISBN-13: 978-1-530-89032-3
ISBN-10: 1-530-89032-2

TABLE OF CONTENTS

PREFACE

This is a revision and update to *Pilgrimage to Personhood*, published in 1987. Over 10,000 copies of that edition sold even though it was never in bookstores. *Pilgrimage to Personhood* was birthed in 1979 when a college and careers group from Austin, Texas invited me to share at their annual retreat. My busy schedule had not allowed me time to prepare for that retreat. The seeds of the ideas presented there were "downloaded" into my spirit as I drove to the retreat center South of Austin that weekend.

The host of that weekend was Bobby Hill, a former student who was working with a college and careers group at the University of Texas. He went on to plant many churches, then he founded Vanguard Ministries in Virginia Beach, Virginia. He is presently pastor of Riverbend Church in Virginia Beach, Virginia. His vision and passion for the kingdom of God have continued to be an inspiration to me.

Many have testified to the value of *Pilgrimage to Personhood* in helping them move to the next level of spiritual and emotional health and wholeness. But my personal understanding of the issues has continued to develop and expand through the decades following that retreat. In this revision I share "the rest of the story."

The first few chapters here are basically the same as the 1987 edition. The changes in language and structure are designed to make it easier to read. The last few chapters reflect a major shift in my understanding of personal identity. I began this journey with the question, "Who am I really?" After years of "upgrades" from Father I now raise a more significant question, "What am I here to do?" My identity is no longer in what I do, but doing is what life is.

T-shirts and Overcoats is about our identity and how it develops, but that theme is only a backdrop to point the way to a deeper level of emotional and spiritual maturity. I use my own personal experiences to illustrate the principles. The imagery of T-shirts and Overcoats is designed to allow the reader to see himself or herself in the story. One thing should be clear from the beginning. This is not a do-it-yourself-kit in self-improvement. It is for those who have given up hope in various self-help techniques.

There is much talk these days about "The Secret" and manifesting what you want. Even though there are many valid principles in the literature, the "True Secret" is still hidden from many who read those books and even from some of those who have written the books. Our goal, as I understand it, is not to manifest what we want but to become who we are by design. That design has very little to do with what you can accumulate or what you can accomplish. In the book of Ecclesiastes Solomon called his many possessions and accomplishments, "vanity of vanities."

This is my story, but it is not intended to be a biography. The imagery is designed to lift the biographical elements out of the purely individual level and place them into the universal human level. Our humanity is our greatest glory and our deepest valley. Which "side" wins out in the end depends on our ability to step outside of our old way of thinking and begin to receive a new way of processing life and relationships. The "heaven and earth" of creation are two sides of created reality. The good news is that we don't have to wait until we die to live on this "other side" of reality. Abundant life here and now is living in "heaven" while we are still on earth.

My study of Greek and Hebrew opened my eyes to see behind our various English versions. As in any translation from one language to another, there are several different words that may be used to indicate the meaning of the text. Every translator uses his or her own understanding to choose which words to use in translating the text. I am no exception. My own insights are reflected in the quotations. Unless otherwise noted the quotations are my own translations, though my understanding is greatly influenced by the Revised Standard Version.

No one is alone when writing. Many have contributed to this material by their responses to the seminars and retreats where this was the theme. Their comments and questions have been a significant formative element in the rewriting of this book.

With gratitude I acknowledge my wife, Lynda, who has had the most influence in my own personal growth. She has been my friend and companion for over 52 years. She also did the proof reading for this book. I love you, Lynda. And I acknowledge my six children. The best way to find out who you really are is to raise a house full of kids. They intuitively know how to train their parents.

I am also grateful for Claire Smith for her help in editing this work and for Ben Patterson who worked with the formatting.

Fount Shults, July, 2016

One: BEING AND BECOMING

Who Am I Really?

The electronics school at Keesler Air Force Base had been in session for several weeks and we had our first weekend off. All of us were ready for a break. Most of my buddies were seeking diversion through partying. My upbringing would not allow me to enjoy the party, but beyond that I wanted to be alone. Some of the basic questions of life were beginning to bubble up into my consciousness. I went to the beach to think. There were other people on the beach but it wasn't crowded. I might just as well have been alone because no one took notice of me. There was a peaceful but eager anticipation in me as if something was on the verge of happening. One never knows what the tide will bring in.

The beach just outside Biloxi, Mississippi was a relaxing place to be. As I waded barefoot in the surf the warm, gentle waves and the movement of the sand under my feet began to calm lingering anxieties. I was alone but I was not lonely. As my mind was quieted my attention began to focus on the inner event which was gradually ebbing its way onto the shore of my awareness.

"It's good to be away from home," I thought. I felt free to be me without having to answer to Dad. I felt I had never been able to please my father no matter how hard I tried. The burden of trying to live up to the expectations of others and feeling so inadequate had taken its toll on my inner development. There on the beach I felt no need to rebel against anything; I just felt a release from pressures I had known all my life. I was free from all that tension, free to become whatever I could become. At least that's what I thought.

Up to this point I had allowed my father to define me and tell me what I should be and what I should become. His focus was on how I fell short. However, with this new sense of freedom new questions began to wash over me like the waves coming in with the tide. "Free to become what?" I asked myself. It was obvious I would never become what Dad wanted me to be. But what *could* I be?

"Maybe there is something like an acorn in me." The thought amused me at first. "The mighty oak is locked up in that little seed. With the right conditions over time the full potential of that acorn will become a reality." The seriousness of the question began to hover overhead like the birds over the seashore. Something was also seeping up from below the surface of my awareness. Hope began to well up within me. "Perhaps there is within me some mysterious kernel waiting for the right conditions to break forth into greatness."

"It's not as simple for people as it is for trees," I reflected. This thought bobbed up from my subconscious heralding a change in my internal 'weather pattern' just as clouds began to form over the sea and the waves began swelling. "What will come from the acorn is predetermined to some degree but a man's destiny is affected by the decisions he makes every day." I mulled that thought over for some time. That other 'something within' which had only been a stirring suddenly acquired a life of its own. These thoughts were new to the surface of my mind but somehow I knew they were not strangers. They had been there in the depths all along.

"What reality is indicated by these thoughts? How significant are they? What is the potential of that life hidden beneath the surf of my awareness?" A sense of excitement emerged as I thought about the possibilities of what I might become. The excitement was countered by a new anxiety as I began to fathom the depths of this new revelation. It occurred to me that I could easily waste my life in frustration trying to become what I was never designed to be, like a pinecone trying to become an oak tree. I realized that I needed to choose my goals according to the way I am designed.

The gulf breeze was becoming a wind. The waves were attacking the shore like an invading band of bandits. Yesterday's answers were no longer satisfying. I wanted something that would help me discover my potential, my destiny. The question arose like a giant that had been sleeping, "Who am I really? Before I decide what I want to become I must first discover who I am by design," I thought.

"I am the son of Bill and Mildred Shults." I was talking to myself under my breath. "Right. But who am I? Who is the 'me' that lives inside this body?"

"One of five children, the second boy," I answered myself. But I realized that my position among the siblings does not define the "who" that I am.

"Yes, but who am I? Who am I in my own right? What can I become?"

"I am a former Art major from The University of New Mexico presently training to be an electronics technician for the United States Air Force." Again I realized that my past accomplishments and my present activity do not define who I am.

3

"That's where I am and what I'm doing, but who is the 'me' that studied art in New Mexico and what will I become as a person?" There seemed to be no answers beyond my identity with my family, my past accomplishments and present involvement with the military. My concern wasn't so much what I might be able to accomplish but who I might become in the process. I was having trouble separating my past involvement and my present activity from my identity.

I had reached the age of asking; I was not yet at the age of finding answers. All I was aware of at that time was a profound sense of becoming, of emerging.

I was alone in the crowd on the beach but I was too overwhelmed to be lonely. I thought I was alone in my questioning. At least it was new to me. But there are always others on the beach where the mystery of the sea of unconsciousness meets the shifting sands of awareness. After many years I have come to realize that these are universal musings which occasionally visit individuals as they begin their life pilgrimage. Not everyone will allow these stirrings to become conscious. Many are threatened by the possibilities of what might be creeping around in the depths of their being, beneath the surface of consciousness.

Some try to avoid awareness by establishing a false identity with the castles they build in the sand, identifying themselves with accomplishments that will not pass the test of the changing tides. Others try to gain significance by following ideas and imaginations that change with each passing generation. Like the mist of the passing clouds these imaginations have no more stability than mere fantasies in flight. The inner man is asleep.

4

The people who try to build their lives in this shifting sand seldom stop to ponder how they came to be on the beach. Or what they will be after the tide returns to challenge their sandcastles. Or when the breeze blows the clouds away. There are casualties on the journey to wholeness. Even so, the possibility of failure must never deter us from moving forward. *Those who hesitate for fear of failure are certain to find the failure they fear.*

On the journey to wholeness—to becoming the person we were born to be—we must always be asking ourselves four basic questions:

(1) Where did I come from?
(2) Where am I going?
(3) What is this world all about and how does it work?
(4) What is my source of strength and direction?

The first is a question of **whence,** i.e. where did I come from. What sort of seed is struggling for survival, what 'word' is striving for expression in my personal journey? The second is a question of **whither,** i.e. where am I going. Is there an ultimate destiny for me, a place of belonging and abiding without striving? We are all looking for a home. Which path do I take from here? The third is a question of **where**, i.e. where am I. What kind of world is this? What are the opposing forces? Is it possible to make things work in this environment?

The fourth is the ultimate question. It is not only about "who am I," but also about **who** or **what** is available to help on this journey? Am I left to myself or is there a guide, a partner for the path? Is there a friend who has gone before and returned to direct me and bring me to that place of wholeness? To ask plainly, "Is there a God? If so who is he and how can I come to know him? *Can He be* my *God*?"

Some of the answers may have been right there waiting for me on that beach but only in a whispering of the breeze. I was ill equipped at that time to recognize the answers or even to understand them even if I had found them. I had lessons to learn and things to go through before I would have ears to hear the answers.

In one sense I was on the right track with my questions. We humans discover who we are and develop our sense of identity through our experiences with the fellow pilgrims with whom we walk as we go toward our destiny. Our self-image develops as others respond to us. Our self-image (not our true self) is bound up with our family, our design, our companions, our perception of the world and our God *as we perceive them.*

In another sense however, I was not on the right track at all. This "*as-we-perceive-them*" changes everything. The direction we choose for our pilgrimage is determined by what we *think* the answers are even if we never consciously ask. By the time we are adults we have long since adopted some basic concepts concerning these fundamental questions of life. It is like we absorbed these by osmosis from our family and cultural environment.

These basic notions are called images because they operate from below the level of consciousness in the imagination. Imagination as we use it here does not refer to fantasy or daydreaming but to the faculty in which pictures of reality develop and through which these unconscious images influence our behavior. These are what the Bible calls "imaginations of the heart." In the

6

Bible the word heart is often related to what we call the unconscious mind.

Few of us are inclined to take the time or make the effort to sit down and articulate our answers to these questions. So we are usually unaware of the influence these images have on our behavior. We continue to fly off the handle and wonder why. We experience anxiety or fear in certain situations for no apparent reason. Those uncontrolled passions regularly return with power and we fall victim to the same ploy again and again. This happens because the most highly charged images (i.e., those urges which are the most difficult to resist) are the ones we are least aware of. We experience them as emotions and we tend to think they happen *to* us as a result of how others treat us. We blame others for our words and actions to avoid taking personal responsibility for our responses.

Our pilgrimage is a journey into dawning awareness but it is not merely an inward journey. To become a whole person with a capacity for abundant life we must become mindful of what is inside us and also of what is out there in the world. So we must not only become conscious of the images which influence our thinking, feeling and aspiring, we must also become aware of the world "out there" as it really is.

This is important because many of our struggles and frustrations are a result of trying to force reality into the form of our images. We come into collision with reality when we try to make things work the way we think they *ought* to work. As a result of this conflict our projects miscarry and something desirable is destroyed as we press toward our inappropriate goals. We seldom stop to consider that perhaps we need to change our *ought*.

If these images are as influential and as significant as we suggest, it becomes supremely important for us to discover and adopt images that are as true to reality as possible. But how can we know who we really are and what the world is really like? The path to wakefulness is not an easy trail to travel because we tend to interpret reality by the unconscious images of our dream-world rather than judging our images by reality (whatever that is). A meaningful life is therefore a life of constant adjustments, of a continuous becoming. *The life which has ceased to adjust has ceased to be meaningful; it has ceased to be life.*

Our goal in this book is to help the reader discover the toxic images which are influencing his or her life and to offer a way out of the old into the new. Our discussion will begin at the beginning—at birth—and will follow the development of the images as the individual grows through various phases of increasing mindfulness.

Most of the illustrations will come from my own experiences, not because of any illusion that my experiences are in any way unique or superior. I use many metaphors to make it easy for each individual to read himself or herself into my story. I present my story simply because I know me best. From time to time I will give attention to the way other personality types may react in similar circumstances. Hopefully most readers will be able to find themselves somewhere in the text, even if it is only between the lines.

Two: T-SHIRTS

The Age of Simply Being

For me it all began in a little rock house in Lovington, New Mexico on a lazy fall day in 1936, September 15 to be exact. It was back in the days when the doctor came to your house to deliver the baby. My father was outside greeting the old country doctor who had come to make his services available on this momentous occasion. The doctor thought he had miscalculated the date. So he and my dad lingered in the front yard.

The greeting drifted into an extended conversation as they continued to enjoy the fresh morning air. They apparently forgot what the doctor had come for until the noise I made came from the open bedroom window. I wanted to attract the attention of the whole neighborhood. I was expressing my disapproval of the fact that they had not been present to witness my arrival.

The doctor rushed into the house, went straight to my mother's bedside and gave me my first medical examination. "Baby boy!" was his official diagnosis. It was easy for him to make that judgment quickly since I was naked at the time. That was not intentional on my part; I was born that way.

No one told me I was supposed to cover up when others were around. I did not know I should be embarrassed. In fact, I was not even aware that there was such a thing as other people in the world. **I was at the age of simply being**. I would learn the art of covering up later. The age of awareness and embarrassment would come in its own time. The others would see to that.

Maturation is a process of increasing levels of awareness or, as some call it, levels of consciousness.

A profound question arises as I think about this first event of my life. If my mother had pinned a pink diaper on me before the doctor arrived would he have pronounced me a baby girl? Certainly not! Doctors look closer than that. What I was wearing or not wearing at the time may have influenced the attitudes of others standing by but it would not have affected what was already there on a basic level even before I was born. What was there I will call *basic nature.* When I speak of the basic nature I include much more than the physical body. I refer to the whole person.

Seed Reproduces after its Kind.

A person is what he is at birth by virtue of what is given through the sperm and the ovum before birth. Many natural abilities, tendencies and potentials are inherited from generations past. (Epigenetics has shown that individual genes "unfold" according to the organism's **perception** of stimulus from the environment in the uterus as well as to the environment after we are born. That means we are at least partly responsible for how we develop as individuals. *A major point in this book is that our **perceptions** are a key to our personal development*.)

Suppose my mother had really wanted a girl. When the doctor left she may have clothed me in dresses with frills, pink lace and fancy shoes. That obviously would not have changed me into a girl. But if she continued over a period of time it would have influenced the way the community of others responded to me. It definitely would have influenced the way I thought about myself (my self-image). But my *basic nature* would have remained the same.

Parents and others put things on children besides diapers. There is such a thing as emotional clothing. In the journey to self-awareness there is an age of receiving and "sinking into" whatever emotional garments are presented by important others (the Greek "put on the new man" pictures "sinking into" an article of clothing). At this early stage of a person's life a person is devoid of the capacity for questioning. Babies do not ask questions; they just observe and respond. Questions come later.

Children believe and receive whatever the primary people in their lives present to them about themselves and about the world. That is what it means to be a child. They are in a receiving mode. Childhood is a vulnerable stage in many ways. Little ones are at the mercy of those who are responsible for their livelihood and training.

Children "put on" (sink into) the self-image that parents offer them in much the same way teens and adults put on T-shirts to identify themselves with a particular group, like a football team or ideological stance. *These images of self will not change the child's nature but they will definitely influence their behavior patterns as they develop and strive to become acceptable as adults.* The tragedy is that children so identify with the T-shirts that they begin to think the T-shirt represents who they really are. This imagined 'real self' often becomes an object of self-hate.

For me it went something like this. One day I looked up at my dad and said to myself, "Wow! That guy is really big. He is the strongest and smartest man in the whole world. He knows everything and can do anything."

As an adult I know there were many men much larger and smarter than my dad. He was only 5' 7" tall. I no longer believe he knew everything or that he could really do more than anyone else. But he was the strongest and smartest man in the world of my childhood.

The point is that our personalities and belief systems develop in the context of *the world as we see it through the eyes of important others in our lives*. Reality is usually different than what we think it is even as adults. But the reality of any given situation is of little significance to our growing individuality. The major contributing factor to our development is *what we **believe** about the way things are*, and we believe according to what is presented to us. (See Bruce Lipton, *Biology of Belief*)

My dad was a building contractor. He had visions of developing a company—he wanted to call it "Shults and Sons"—so he was pleased that I was a boy. The problem of having to wear the dresses and lace of femininity was a non-issue. So far so good. But the boy I was did not match the boy he dreamed about. He wanted a guy who would be good at hands-on things.

He expected me to become an ideal carpenter's son. To achieve that he continually applied pressure. He tried to put something on me that did not fit. He was probably as frustrated by trying to get me to perform as I was trying to please him. When I tried to wear it I soon discovered I would probably never be able to fill the "Master Carpenter" T-shirt he had designed for me. The fact that I did not fit the shirt convinced me that there was something wrong with the '*am*' I was born with.

It never occurred to me that there might be something

wrong with Dad's expectations. He was the guy who knew everything. He would not expect something of me I should not be able to do. No little boy would suspect his father had faulty expectations. In my mind there was something seriously wrong with *me*. I knew (imagined) it was my own inadequacies that were to blame. If Mom had wanted me to be a girl, and if I had tried to become what she wanted, the level of my frustration would not have been any greater than what came from trying to please Dad. It just was not in my nature to become a master carpenter.

My journey into self-awareness was complicated further by the omnipresence of a big brother who had what it takes to be a master carpenter. Joe was one who liked to take charge and do whatever needed to be done. It was like his hands always knew what to do. I was the kind who had to understand all the "hows" and "whys" before I began a project. But by the time I understood how and why my motivation had been fully satisfied. I had no interest in doing anything about it.

When Dad would give us simple assignments to work on, like sweeping sawdust or pulling nails out of boards, my brother would simply do it while I was trying to figure out how and why. He ended up doing most of the work without taking time to explain things to me.

Now it was fine with me for him to do everything. That gave me more time to analyze the process and consider the meaning of it all. (I learned much later that analyzing and processing things mentally was more like the real me than the hands-on carpenter.) But when Dad came back to inspect our work, Joe did not hesitate to make it clear who had done all the work.

"Fount does not know how to do anything," he would declare. "He just stood around daydreaming the whole time." I adopted his perspective of me. That is what many do at this stage of development. We accept other's assessment of who we are.

"You should know how to do that." Dad was always very sure about what I should be able to do. "How many times do I have to tell you? You are just dumb; that's all, just dumb," he would say.

There it was, the first article of clothing for my developing self-concept. This "Dumb-Dumb" T-shirt seemed to fit much better than the "Master Carpenter" shirt. So I put it on. *I sank into that self-image.*

"You could do as well as your brother," Dad would say, "if only you would apply yourself. You should know how to do that."

He was right as far as I could tell. I looked at my T-shirt and it all made sense. A Dumb-Dumb should know but he does not. That is what it means to be dumb. Thus with bowed head and tear dampened cheeks I entered the age of self-awareness wearing my Dumb-Dumb T-shirt.

During the next few months several other words and phrases were added to my T-shirt.

'Lazy.' I sewed it on as soon as possible.

'Never-will-amount-to-anything.' I liked that one. It sounded exciting because it had lots of letters in it. I put it on in many different colors.

In all this business of discovering who I was "supposed to be" and comparing it to what I really was I never stopped to notice the T-shirt was an identity *put on me from outside*. Since I was still immature the T-shirt obviously fit well. I really was dumb and inadequate

14

compared to Dad and Joe. They understood how to do things and did them better and faster. I had no reason to doubt the words on the T-shirt. *The words were an accurate picture of the self-concept I developed as a result of my father's words and my brother's ability.*

I later became aware of other young ones like myself who were also wearing T-shirts. The community of big people had arranged a situation where we could get to know one another. It was a large stone building with the words *"Grammar School"* over the entrance. I did not understand what that meant but it soon became clear what we were all there for. We were supposed to learn how to play the role indicated on our T-shirts. My place in life was to be the Dumb-Dumb so I had to learn how to be dumb in as many situations as possible. I knew I could do it. I could be as dumb as the best of them.

It is amazing how well we little ones were able to read one another's T-shirts long before we could read what was written in books. It was not terribly bothersome to me when other kids noticed I was dumb. That was all I had known since the light of self-awareness had first begun to glow. The light was still quite dim so I didn't know I should be ashamed of being dumb. *I had not reached the age of social awareness.*

My first day in class was unforgettable. One guy was there with a "Trouble-Maker" T-shirt. He was there to learn how to run over others and get his own way. He never seemed to notice that others had feelings. In the very back of the room was a little fellow with "Timid" written on his T-shirt. His project was to learn how to receive abuse without coming into open conflict. It was exciting to discover how their roles could interact when those two got together.

Next to me was a girl with a "Charming" T-shirt. She had already learned how to use her charm to her best interest. She only needed to sharpen her ability to lure and entice without getting herself into a situation where she would actually have to pay for what she wanted. It was obvious she would do well in adult life.

There was "Cry-Baby." She got what she wanted by crying until even the teacher had to give in. And there was "I-am-always-right" who never allowed others to win an argument. There were many others we could mention, but you have probably already met most of them.

During the first few weeks I discovered that the teacher did not understand what we were there for. She seemed to think we wanted to learn how to read and write and play with numbers. At first this disturbed me because if I learned all those things it would destroy my self-image. Then it occurred to me. That environment was perfect to demonstrate my short-comings. Since I was dumb no one would expect me to do well so I decided to go for it.

My big brother had been sick during his first year of school and had to repeat the first grade. We were close enough in age for me to join him his second time through. This worked out for both of us. He already understood most of the material so he spent his time doing my homework for me. This was good for him because he was learning how to use his "I-Can-Do-It-Better-Than-You" T-shirt to increase his self-esteem. It was good for me because *I was learning how to avoid work by being dumb*.

In our third year together the teacher called my mother in for a conference. "Fount's a smart boy," she said, "but he will never learn to do his own work as long as he is in the same class as Joe." They agreed that I should be held back a year.

Now I was on my own. I would have to prove I was dumb without Joe's help. I was confident I would be able to do it especially since I could add to my credentials the fact that I had repeated third grade. For the next few years Joe continued to do my homework for me at home. He felt he needed more experience proving he could "do it better" before he graduated into adult life. This served a double purpose for me. I was able to satisfy the teachers and maintain my integrity as a dumb-dumb at the same time.

Seed and Received Word

Another question arises at this point. Why did I feel obligated to prove I was dumb? Why was I not able to accept the teacher's evaluation and think of the set-back as an opportunity to prove I was smart? As it turns out the teacher's assessment was correct since I was able to complete my education through post-graduate work. Why could I not see that? The answers to these questions will become clear as we continue our journey together.

The **basic nature** of a child is "given" before birth and we will call the agent of that nature **seed**. In using the term seed we imply more than what is supplied by the sire together with the ovum. We refer to all that comes to an individual through the process of generation, through both the mother and the father. *Seed in this sense reaches all the way back to primal man* (called "Adam" in the Bible).

By the term "basic nature" we refer to human nature

as it finds specific expression in each particular individual. This is the reality of what a person "is" whether he or she is consciously aware of it or not. (See fig. #1)

In the context of developing self-awareness, the agent that forms the self-image is the **word received** like a T-shirt from important others. By the term "word" we imply more than the mere verbiage which is spoken in the child's hearing. We refer to all levels and forms of communication coming from one's parents, siblings, classmates and the community. This includes both verbal and non-verbal communication. Verbal communication happened when Dad said I was dumb. The non-verbal variety occurred when Joe did everything before I could figure out how or why.

The Age of Receiving

Each of us begins life with a basic nature – the root from which all development sprouts. The first stage of development we call the **age of receiving**. Just as the ovum receives the sperm, so a child receives words (actually spoken or only implied) as seeds that provide images of meaning. During this time our self-image (as distinct from our basic nature) takes form. This formation evolves in the context of the interactions between our basic nature and important others in our lives. As the word is given and received the self-image takes form and becomes firmly established. As long as we continue to receive the same words the self-image will remain unchanged. This is the case even when we are speaking it to ourselves in our self-talk.

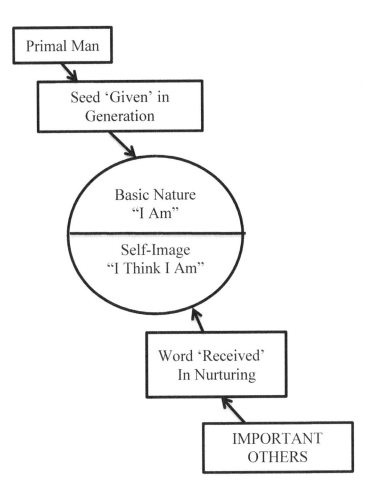

Figure #1 Nature and Nurture

The word "*receive*" is very important in this context. We are not suggesting that the self-image can never change while the same attitudes and expressions of others remain the same. The formative element is the word as the child **receives** it, not necessarily the way parents and others offer it. *What the child receives can be quite different from what parents intend.* My dad was actually trying to encourage me by using negative motivation.

When the parents attempt to encourage and give affirmation the child is often discouraged and feels shame. But there should come a time of maturity when the child is able to disregard inappropriate words of communication from others even when they *intend* to produce shame and condemnation. Those *received words* inhibit our development and our ability to perform well. *When the old word is **no longer received** one is free to experience change and begin to manifest the reality of who he is by design.* Later we will discuss ways to facilitate that maturity for any who are ready for change.

We must also give attention to the part one's basic nature plays in the development of the self-image. My particular nature, being more docile than resistant, led me to submit to the image of "Dumb-Dumb" and find ways to demonstrate how dumb I could be. Someone more aggressive, like my brother Joe, would resist the negative image and set out to prove it false. Even in that case however, the "Dumb-Dumb" image is still a formative element. As long as he is trying to prove he is not dumb it is evident he has received the word "dumb" as a threat.

We arrive at a higher level of maturity (more aware, more fully awake and mindful) when we are able to disregard the words and actions of others and are no longer triggered by those words. We also begin to manifest our true nature as we overcome the inhibitions caused by the received word. *A boy becomes a man when he no longer needs to prove he is a man.* He is then able to develop according to what he is in-and-of-himself with no concern about what others think.

The Age of Confirmation

We call the second stage of development the **age of confirmation**. We tend to interpret situations and statements in terms of the word we have already received (or rejected). For me the prior word was "Dumb-Dumb." I thought I was dumb so I interpreted everything as proving that fact. Any event or situation that could not be pressed into the framework of that prior word I simply ignored or interpreted to mean I was dumb.

An aggressive person, having rejected the title "Dumb-Dumb," might respond in anger to statements if he thought the words implied he was dumb – even when that was not the speaker's intent. Or he would study harder to prove he is not dumb. His anger and intensity would expose the fact that he felt threatened. His study habits would indicate he felt a need to prove his intelligence against what he perceives as a threat. In either case he is really reacting against the important other in his childhood who said he was dumb.

In this phase we also learn how to manipulate others to have proof of the validity (or invalidity) of the prior word. We intentionally (though unconsciously) do things to elicit a response we can use to confirm or deny the image we have received. Usually we are totally unaware of what we are doing. When others accuse us of trying to manipulate we deny it. Otherwise we would have to admit we are living a lie. So we (unconsciously) lie on purpose.

One example of this is that I let my brother know I did not understand something so he would do my homework for me. I was not aware of what I was doing. But what better way could I prove my stupidity and maintain my self-image? For that matter what better way could my brother prove he did know more? As long as he continued to do all the work I would never have to learn how and he would become more and more experienced.

As stated earlier, we do this unconsciously. B*ut it is this unconscious aspect that gives the images their power.* If I had been consciously aware of what I was doing I might have tried to resist giving the impression I was dumb. But since the image was unconscious I did not know it was false. I also did not know I might be able to resist its power. *It was not until I became aware of the existence of the image that I began to gain mastery over it.* I would have to pass through several stages of development before I would come to that point in my life.

The next stage of development I call the **age of longing**. During this stage we try to find our place within the social structure beyond the family and close friends. *This is a time of searching for identity within a group.* It is a time of peer pressure and a time of striving to find a way to be special in the eyes of someone 'out there' where we find ourselves in the social system. It is a time of wondering what adult life will be like and a time of vacillating between wanting to be an adult and wanting to remain a child.

As we develop from one stage to another we are in

the process of becoming. On the one hand our 'being' is never static because we are endlessly changing as we move forward. But there is something that never changes, namely our basic nature, who we really are. We might do better to speak of ourselves as "*humans-in-the-process-of-becoming*" rather than human *beings*. As we change we do not become something other than human. We simply find new and different ways of expressing our humanity. Sometimes we are *inhuman (or toxic) in our behavior.* But even that does not change us to something other than human.

In every stage we continue to develop according to the words we receive as "meaning-seeds" which will produce the next level of our understanding of our identity and our place in the world. And, as we have noted, it does not matter whether the words are actually spoken or only implied, whether the important other actually meant it or we misinterpreted it.

In the next chapter we turn to the question of how we begin to cover up what we think is the true self.

Three: CLOWN SUITS AND CLOSETS

Longing for Belonging

Boy was I ever surprised the first time I entered the new school building! I had been excited all summer. Students who had already been through that building said we would all begin to look like adults. The teachers there would train us to act like grownups. Over the doors were the words *Middle School*. I could hardly wait.

"Just think, Li'l Dumb-Dumb becoming an adult!"

The first day of school I arrived with my Dumb-Dumb T-shirt all washed and clean. What a shock when I looked around at my friends. Someone had warned the others that things would be different in Middle School. Most of them weren't showing their old T-shirts. They were covering them with more acceptable slogans. "Trouble-maker" was wearing a football jersey with "Hero" written on the front. "Timid" was wearing dark glasses and a black jacket with "Cool" on the front and back. Miss "Charming" was wearing high heels with a blouse labeled "High-Class." As I looked at those who had not yet covered their T-shirts the bright light of social awareness caused the luster of the old familiar slogans to fade. I looked at my own T-shirt and felt more ashamed than ever over being dumb.

Things were changing so rapidly I did not know what to do. *I was unaware of the possibility that the Dumb-Dumb was not the **real** me*. I had totally identified with the words Dad had spoken over me. It would have eased the pain if I had remembered what it was like back behind

24

the veil of clouded memories when I was just *me* with no T-shirt.

It was no longer appropriate to allow my T-shirt to be seen in public. Everyone made fun of those who had not yet covered themselves. We were all threatened by the possibility of our undershirts being exposed in the new light of social awareness.

"If I continue to wear my T-shirt people will know who I really am," I thought. It still did not occur to me that the slogans on the shirts could be removed. No, I would have to cover mine like everyone else. Thus I entered the **age of social awareness** looking for an appropriate cover-up for my poor self-image. *I was longing to belong.*

The Clown Suit

At first I was confused by the fact that teachers, preachers and parents were allowed to express their feelings but we little ones were not. Then I got it. The big people already had their certificate of adulthood and did not have to prove themselves anymore, at least not to the little people. They had collected enough tokens to demand acceptance the way they were.

*One of the main objectives of this phase of training was to select and assume a **false identity**.* We must learn to cover our true feelings before we could receive a certificate of adulthood. Letting others know how we actually felt inside was strictly forbidden. Somehow we had to pretend to be something other than what we were and collect tokens of acceptance at the same time. I did not realize until many years later that the Dumb-Dumb was also a false-identity.

Within the various peer groups we continued to help one another with our goals. We took turns doing and saying ugly things to one another to see if we could cause the other to drop his cover and expose his T-shirt. We were gaining experience maintaining our false identity in the face of tremendous pressures. The T-shirts were being buried so far beneath the surface that it would be a long time before we would have courage to ask ourselves the basic question, "Who am I really?" Some never would.

"What can a dummy do to cover up and avoid exposing his stupidity?" The question haunted me until I remembered something. In all my experiences of learning how to do dumb things I had come to enjoy making people laugh. The fabric of the dummy was easy to rework into a new uniform. I came to school the next day dressed in my "Clown-Suit" to cover the "Dumb-Dumb."

My particular disguise offered a decided advantage during this phase. I could conceal my embarrassment behind funny antics and spontaneous skits. With everyone laughing no one would notice that I really was dumb. My ace-in-the-hole was that if ever I actually did something dumb (which I often did) I could cover up by pretending I did that on purpose to make people laugh. This ploy was adequate for those who would accuse me of exposing my T-shirt.

This masquerade offered me a second advantage. It gave me the *illusion* of being accepted in the group. Everyone enjoys laughing so I was always welcome in the various gatherings. I was especially welcome in situations where the big people were putting pressure on us. I could always come up with some funny remark or go through some comical routine and break up the tension. That often got me in trouble with adults but the positive attention of my peers was worth it.

Once we became convinced that we must always keep our underwear covered no matter what the cost, the light of self-awareness grew even brighter. Each of us began to concentrate on himself and covering his own inadequacies. The memory of the others' T-shirts had completely faded by this time. Each of us thought he was the only one pretending. Everyone else seemed to be completely satisfied with themselves and their abilities. No one suspected I was dissatisfied with me because I was also one of the pretenders.

The Brass Doors

For our final stage of preparation for adult life they moved us to another building. This one had *"High School"* over the entrance. At the other end of this building there were two huge Brass Doors through which we would be allowed to pass if we proved ourselves worthy. They told us that the real world was on the other side of those doors. In the center of this structure was a large room full of books and study desks. They said we would never make it in the real world if we did not learn what was in those books.

When they described the real world it sounded more like a very big and efficient business office where the only important thing was to make a profit. From the way they talked I had trouble figuring out whether the medium of exchange would be knowledge or money. In time I finally understood that money was the ultimate token of acceptability and knowledge was the means to that end. Then I realized something. I would not have to be a master carpenter if I could learn what was in those books.

As I stood in that room with huge stacks of books looming before me like a well-guarded castle, chills went through my innermost parts. Everything I needed to know to be successful was locked securely behind the covers of those books. Everyone knows that dummies do not have a key to unlock the mysteries hidden on those shelves. My clown suit would be useless in the attempt to discover the secrets concealed in books.

"A Dumb-Dumb can never succeed in a task as foreboding as this." I thought. "How will I ever be able to make it in the world out there beyond the Brass Doors?"

The prospect of entering a world for which I was so ill-equipped caused me to spend much time in despondency wishing the world was different. I knew (at least I thought I knew) I could never be different. I was longing for some utopian world in which people like me could have a place of significance. My self-image was only one problem now. *The new "image problem" is our our idea of what the world is like.*

The Effects of False Images

Our problem is that *we respond to the world according to what we imagine it to be rather than what it really is*. The truth is that the world is different from the world-image we developed in childhood and High School. The world is undoubtedly different from our image of it even in adult life. (Quantum physics is changing our perceptions.) Just as the real me is quite different from the image I had of myself, so the world is also quite different from the teen-age images. Only a small portion of the world is correctly represented by the image of a business office.

The teachers obviously talked about many other aspects of life and how it would be after graduation. My own insecurities and low self-esteem focused on the things I thought I would never be able to do. The feelings were an interface of my self-image and my world-image. The truth is that there is a place for all of us in the real world. The problem was all in my imaging faculty. My anxiety and longing could have been avoided if I had understood that my false-self was reacting to *an image of the world* rather than to the *real world*.

During this age of longing I was so busy trying to gather tokens of acceptance that I seldom stopped to notice that I was really lonely. The loneliness came from relating to others superficially through the false identity. As the "Class-Clown" I had friends who related to me on that basis but the clown was not the real me. Most of the time I was satisfied with the *illusion of acceptance.* But when I suspected it was an illusion the fear of being completely cut off from my peers moved me to continue clowning so I would feel accepted.

A much deeper longing arose when the question came up from the subterranean caverns within. "*Does anyone like me just for me*? If I didn't make them laugh would anyone still accept me?" This longing for intimacy was totally suppressed at that time, of course. At that point I did not even realize the acceptance was not real. *I had only tokens with very little reality.* A brighter light would have to shine before I would be able to see this.

This stage is not limited to a chronological age

bracket. Many get trapped here and are unable to move on. They get caught in a holding pattern for years before they are able to break out. Some never gain enough courage to allow the question to rise into conscious thought. The prospect of a negative answer is too threatening. It is a fearful thing to be "cut off from the land of the living." This binds to a life of continuing to make available what we *have* or what we *can do* in exchange for the illusion of acceptance. This bondage remains until we realize the tokens have no real value.

With the Brass Doors clearly in view we began to turn our attention to the future. Peer relationships were still important, but the tokens were now being awarded according to what one planned to be when he or she graduated. This change of pace seemed to help suppress the feelings of inadequacy for most of the students. Still many of us saw others as having more potential. Some covered their feelings of being defective with great plans for the future. At best each saw his or her own potential as less than the image he or she wanted to present to others.

I looked at those shelves full of books again. I knew I would never be able to become anything important, so I set my goal just to get through the Brass Doors. If I could do that it would be quite an accomplishment for a Dumb-Dumb. I knew I must get through or be exposed as dumb. The pressures continued to mount. I had serious doubts that I would be able to make it. But I never let anyone else know. I had become *the great pretender*.

There was also the struggle of trying to keep up the image of "Class-Clown" when other pressures were so great. I thought about taking off the clown suit to concentrate on study. But if I studied and still failed then everyone would know I was dumb. The only pleasurable feelings I had in those days was having others laugh at my impromptu skits. All my peers enjoyed my humor and seemed to like me as long as I was being funny.

"That's nice," I thought, "but would they like me if they knew the real me, if they knew how dumb I really am?"

The most important thing in my life at that time was for the "real me" to be loved and accepted as I was rather than for what I could do. In the privacy of my heart I still suspected that the others did not really like me. *They only liked the good feeling they had while they were laughing at my antics.* They loved themselves and their good feelings. But I had learned to depend on my sense of humor to collect tokens of acceptance. Even though I had a feeling those tokens were counterfeit I continued to collect them. The only alternative seemed to be no tokens at all. That would be a fate worse than death.

The Closet

Each day the prospect of my T-shirt being exposed was increasing. Retreat seemed the only sensible course of action. A more aggressive person might have intensified his efforts in sports or academics. I found a "closet" in the room with all the books. It was a very special kind of closet where to anyone looking in from outside of my little world I appeared to be studying. Inside this closet I could enjoy very exciting adventures.

When I needed company I would draw pictures of very a handsome young man with big muscles and pretty girls who obviously needed a strong man's attention. I would become the muscle-man and fall madly in love with the girl. She would always get herself in a situation of great danger and I would come save her. This usually required incredible speed, super feats of strength and sometimes even the ability to fly. With the girl's eternal affection I felt important. It felt good to be needed even if it was only in my imagination.

One day I decided to come out of my closet and try my hand with a real girl. I chose the one who sat in front of me in class. I whispered her name and asked, "Do you love me?"

"No." She answered very simply.

"Do you like me?" I was only looking for some positive response from someone outside my closet.

"No." Her answer did not indicate even the slightest interest in the direction of my questions. At that point I really needed some kind of response to reassure me I had some reason for being around.

"Do you hate me?" I waited for an answer. I would have been satisfied with a "yes" answer. That would at least indicate that I was the object of real attention from someone out there.

"Quite frankly," she responded very calmly, "I never give you a thought one way or the other."

I quickly scampered back into my closet. It would be a long time before I would venture out again.

I seldom used the clown suit any more except for occasional social encounters. I spent most of my time in my closet so the disguise was no longer important. When the day was over I would move quietly toward the exit with little attention to others. I limited my conversations to the necessary social exchanges like "See you later."

Fear of Separation

The formative element during this age of longing for belonging is a power called separation anxiety. This type of anxiety is experienced in infancy and later in the teen years. As we enter the process of separating from our parents (a necessary separation for wholeness) we vacillate between wanting to be dependent and wanting to be independent. Our attention in this stage is on our relationship with our peers rather than our parents.

This fear is related in many ways to the fear of death. In the Old Testament there is both a positive and a negative attitude toward death depending on the condition of the one who is dying. On the positive side there is the notion of the righteous person who merely changed their place of belonging from the living community to the sleeping community. The phrase, "sleep with the fathers," was used to indicate this notion.

Death was not a fearful thought for those who were confident of being received into the loving community of those who were asleep. Among the Hebrew people there was no fear of death for those righteous people who were confident that there would be no separation from the larger community which included the dead. *The issue for them wasn't death as such; it was separation*. The fear of death, then, is the fear of ending up with no place in the community. This confidence is reflected in Isaiah 57:1-2:

"The righteous man perishes, and no one takes notice; devout men are removed while no one understands. For the righteous man is taken away from disaster; he enters into peace; they rest in their beds who walk in their uprightness."

Notice the phrase *"rest in their beds."* This positive notion was reflected in the burial practices of Israel. Jacob insisted that his bones be taken from Egypt back to the land of Canaan after his death so he could be with his fathers in their bed (Genesis 47:30). David "slept with his fathers" (I Kings 2:10). And Hezekiah was buried in the "chiefest tombs of the sons of David." His grave-bed was next to his great-grandfather David.

The negative side of this notion is often expressed by the phrase "cut off from the living." We can illustrate this notion by the burial practices also. Manasseh, the most wicked king in the history of Judah, was not allowed the honor of sleeping with his fathers. He was buried in his own house – alone (II Chronicles 33:20). For him there was a separation from the community at death. The reason Jezebel had no burial at all was to indicate that she was completely cut off at death. She wasn't even allowed a resting place among the wicked.

The Power of Death

The concept of death we are introducing here is not physical death as such but social isolation and rejection. We see the power of this fear of separation in the effect it has on our behavior. We often do things we know are wrong just to avoid social isolation. So now we turn our attention to the *power of rejection and its influence on our lives in the face of a threat of social separation.*

34

The fear of separation operates the same as the fear of death. The Israelites feared separation during life as much as death itself, perhaps more so. The confident affirmation of Psalm 49:15, "But God will ransom my soul from the power of Sheol," illustrates this. The psalmist was not implying that God would keep him from the inevitability of dying. He knew that everyone would face the reality of death at some point. He expected to be ransomed from the *POWER* of death.

The power of Sheol in this psalm is related to the fear of separation. That is clear from the context. This distinction between physical death and the fear of separation becomes clear in Ruth Paxton's book *Life on the Highest Plane.* She quoted Mrs. McDonough, "Death is the falling out of correspondence with environment." Death is separation from the environment in which life has its relationships, vitality and meaning. This is true of all life systems.

To illustrate: A leaf has its life and significance within the environment by virtue of its relationship with the tree, the sun and the atmosphere. It finds its meaning in the operation of receiving light from the sun, carbon dioxide from the air and in giving oxygen into the air. When the freeze comes the leaf does not cease to exist but it no longer corresponds with the atmosphere and the tree. It dies, i.e., it is separated from its relationships and enters into a new relationship with the soil as a nutrient.

So the essential element in death is separation. The larger context of Psalm 49 does not present a battle in which the physical life of the psalmist was threatened. His problem was the threat of men who trust in their wealth (v. 6). There was apparently a feeling of being separated

35

or rejected on basis of the small measure of the psalmist's possessions. The fear of separation was produced by comparing his financial situation with the wealthy.

The New Testament also speaks of the power of death. Hebrews speaks of Jesus partaking of our nature so that "through death he might destroy the one who has the power of death, that is, the devil, and deliver all those who through fear of death were subject to lifelong slavery" (Hebrews 2:14, 15). Notice the text doesn't speak of physical death as such, but of the *power of death* that comes through fear. This *fear of separation* causes a *lifelong bondage*.

Deliverance from the fear of death comes with the assurance that there will be no alienation in the death/separation experience. One who is confident of being received into a more significant community has no fear of separating from the one he is now associated with. For example: Moving from a low paying job with poor working conditions to a job with good pay and people who get along with one another isn't threatening. Being fired with no prospect of another job is fearful.

The Power of Sheol

The context of Psalm 49 reveals the state of affairs that brought the psalmist to fear. In that situation we also find a hint of how a person might come under the "*power of Sheol*" in the first place. After a call for the reader to listen the palmist said in verses 5 and 6, "Why should I fear in times of trouble, when the iniquity of those who cheat, those who trust in their wealth and boast of the abundance of their riches?" The question indicates he was actually experiencing fear even though he knew the fear was unfounded. That will become clear as we continue.

It's easy to understand how one would have negative emotions while being surrounded by people who arrogantly flaunt their wealth. But we wouldn't normally identify those negative feelings as fear unless there was more to it than mere boasting. The wealthy were obviously using their wealth as a means of *excluding the psalmist from their circle* of friends. So the psalmist's fear is related to rejection, separation or isolation. The rich were using their wealth to feel good about themselves at the expense of those with less.

This brings us to our point. The phrase "power of Sheol" is related to the fear of rejection and abandonment. The particular form of wealth the persecutors possessed is not essential for the point. *The psalmist felt rejected from the "in" crowd because of something he didn't have.* His negative feelings can thus be identified as fear, more specifically the fear of rejection and isolation. It is not a physical grave the psalmist fears; it's a *fear of being left out.*

In the Hebrew language Sheol refers to the grave but in poetry it often refers to what we often call depression or being "in the pits." Encouragement came to the psalmist when he realized *God would receive* him. *God redeemed him from the power of rejection, abandonment and depression by receiving him into his presence* (Psalms 49:15). The fear was defeated when he realized he was received into a more significant relationship.

When we expand the view of wealth to include anything one might consider of value, anything one might use to have an advantage over others, then we understand how the power of Sheol operates. In one group it might be a new car or a bigger house. In another group it might be better grades or a position of authority.

My big brother had a form of wealth that I valued highly as we were growing up. He had our father's positive attention and approval. That in itself was not a problem but he often used that as a means of exalting himself at my expense. I fell into the pit of despair and self-condemnation. I felt inferior and worthless. *Gripped by the power of Sheol* I was in a lifelong bondage.

This exposes the subtle devices of the one who has the power of death through the fear of death (Hebrews 2:14, 15). When we receive negative communication from important others in our youth we begin to see ourselves as inferior in one way or another. This becomes a problem when peer relationships become an important element in the formation of our self-concept. The power of Sheol begins to exert its secret, destructive influence.

First, each one of us sees the others (whichever group we want to be a part of, but we are not) as having something of value that we do not have. The "possession" that gives the others an advantage becomes the goal in our lives, but because of our low self-esteem we see their advantage as something we can never have. We begin to wallow in the pit of despair (which the Bible calls Sheol). It becomes a lifelong bondage until we deal with it.

It is like an unwritten law in the social world of teens: *The supreme penalty of being different is to be cut off from the 'in' crowd.* Those of the 'in' crowd appear to us to be really living. To be separated from the 'living' is a fate worse than physical death. For fear of experiencing separation many young people begin to do things they would never otherwise do, things that could even kill them. That is the power of Sheol. That is bondage.

The result of the attempt to conform—for which the person may secretly condemn himself—is that he begins to close himself off from the voice of his conscience. *He would rather face the pressures of guilt than to face the prospect of being isolated from the "in" group.* He may develop superficial relationships in which he exchanges counterfeit tokens of acceptance for the illusion of being accepted.

He may be aware that he is not really accepted but he will bury that awareness beneath the cover of the behavior the group uses to control those who belong. In so doing— and here is the subtlety of Sheol's power—he has chosen to believe a lie and to try to live by that lie. The lie comes like a seed to an 'ovum of the soul' to produce a life of deception. When one is under the influence of the *Lie of Sheol*, separation from men and women of the 'in' group seems to have more serious consequences than separation from the Source of true life.

Those who follow this course to its end will find that the superficial relationships are built in the sand and will be washed away by the returning tide. If he ever tries to do something different from the approving crowd a boy (or young woman) will discover that the tokens are only tokens. He was never really accepted for who he really is anyway. Having compromised his conscience, betrayed his personal integrity and surrendered his honor, he will also find he is alienated from himself. This is a fate worse than death.

Each stage begins in a transition *from what we were* and moves toward *what we are becoming*. In each transition we are again in a receiving mode. We can choose to continue to believe the lies, we can receive and try to live by new lies, or we can wake up to what has been happening and begin to receive truth. Lies open us to a life of frustration, anxiety and depression where alienation rules. Truth opens us to a life of healthy involvement in a community where love rules.

We were created to seek and to have close intimate relationships. When we seek close relationships within a group which is dominated by lies, we have made a bad choice. (M. Scott Peck calls this group the "*The People of the Lie*." The prospect of facing life alienated from the chosen group sets up an inner dynamic that begins to drive us to seek approval at any cost. If there is no approval within the chosen group, we will be in torment until we find another place of belonging.

Striving to find a place of belonging by behaving in a way that is not consistent with our basic nature causes us to become an expression of something we are not. We develop a false image of ourselves and identify that image as our true nature. This is a false-self. It is what Paul called the "old man" which must die. The "new man" is the one we are designed to become; it is the one created in the image of God, the one He knit together in the mother's womb.

In the next chapter we shift our attention to the inner working of this dynamic.

Four: THE BIG TREEHOUSE

My New World-Image

The final year of our training finally came to an end. I was ready to go through the Brass Doors into the real world. I was unsure of what to expect out there but was nevertheless eager to leave the room with all those books. I was certain I would become a complete failure, but I wanted out. I had to graduate.

The schoolmasters provided appropriate suits for all of us to wear at the graduation ceremony. They gave us long maroon robes so none of our T-shirts would show. On the front of the robes were the words, "I Have Arrived." They also gave us specially made caps to wear. Attached to the top of the cap was a string we were to pull as we crossed the stage to go toward the Brass Doors.

When we pulled the string a flashing light would appear with a flag saying, "SUCCESS." I knew I had not succeeded at anything but I was not willing to be exposed at that time. When they called my name I walked across the stage, received my diploma, pulled the string and went through the Brass Doors as though everything was cool, as though I had really accomplished something.

After graduating from High School I discovered that things on the other side of the Brass Doors were much different from what we had been told. It was a jungle instead of a business office and the law was the survival of the fittest. It was not knowledge but hardness that brought in the profits. They were right about one thing; the appearance of having money was the ultimate symbol of success, the most precious token of acceptability.

The question of how much a person is worth was given in terms of assets and liabilities. One's abilities were not judged by what they could actually do but by how many tokens came in at the box office. Since money was such a symbol *those who had more used it to enslave those who wanted more*. Most were not aware they were slaves; they thought having a job meant they were free. Yet none of them thought they were being paid enough, so they worked harder to receive more. They were slaves to their jobs.

The means to acceptability was not knowledge; it was a combination of cleverness, aggression and a thing called grit. I was sure I had none of those things. All I had was a clown suit, a photograph of me wearing the robe of success and a certificate they handed me as I walked toward the Brass Doors. The photo was already fading in the heat of the jungle and I could not remember where I put the certificate that said I was a jungle-faring man.

I began looking for a treehouse with a clown's position open. There was no demand for clowns in the jungle unless one wanted to travel with the circus. That prospect had only a slight attraction for me. The idea of making people laugh while the man with a cane and a big cigar took their money did not appeal to me at all. I enjoyed clowning in spontaneous situations, but the thought of wearing it permanently was not attractive to me at all.

It seemed everyone else had enough money to buy all those nice things that make you look successful. There I was with nothing, no tokens and no way of collecting any. I learned later that most of the others were in debt for all their symbols of acceptability. No one ever told anyone else how many tokens he actually had. They just bought as many shiny things as the token masters (the slave owners) would allow. They seldom took their eyes off their stuff long enough to notice that they had become slaves of the token masters.

The pretense and cover-up of the early teen years continued in the adult world. Those who learned to play the game well gathered many symbols of success. Some tried to play honestly; others cheated regularly. But winning was everything for those who were in the system. The power of the token masters had bewitched them into thinking that winning was more important than integrity and friendship. The rule was that one is not dishonest or unfriendly unless he gets caught with his T-shirt exposed.

Dumb-Dumb in College

Discovering the world beyond the Brass Doors to be a vicious place was a disheartening experience. I was about to despair when my sister and brother-in-law offered to provide an interest free loan for me to go to college. I appreciated the offer. It encouraged me but I was threatened by the prospect of being a college student.

"A Dumb-Dumb is certain to be exposed in a university," I pondered, "but here in the jungle I will not only be exposed I will be eaten alive."

I decided to accept their offer but did not tell them how threatened I felt. As I looked more closely at the university I found a place where it might be possible for me to hide. In the closet of my imagination during high school I had learned to draw well enough to think I might be able to make it through college as an Art major at the University of New Mexico.

"Art majors are not expected to have a key to unlock the secrets in the books," I reassured myself. "Besides, with my brother-in-law paying the expenses, I will not have to face the issue of collecting the green certificates of success for quite some time yet."

As soon as I arrived on campus I bought a pair of dark glasses, let my hair grow a bit and tried to produce a beard with the five whiskers that appeared on my chin. I wore an old pair of jeans and a worn out sweatshirt with the word "Beat" on the front and back. The Beat generation was perhaps worse than the Hippies who came later. At least the Hippies seemed to be more open and honest about their true feelings than Beatniks were.

Much to my surprise when I went through registration they insisted that all freshmen were required to take certain courses regardless of their major. They did not believe me when I explained that Art majors would only need to learn to draw and paint. I lost the argument (Boy did I feel dumb!) and they saddled me with several classes that would require study and library work. I quickly pulled my torn sweatshirt over the exposed T-shirt and pranced out as though I expected to succeed.

In addition to the basic Art requirements I took French, History and English Literature. I was able to drift through French with very little effort and convince the professor that I knew enough French to get a relatively good grade.

"What a dumb professor," I thought. "Imagine giving a good grade to a Dumb-Dumb."

History and English were different. The university

library was much worse than anything I had ever seen in high school. It was several stories high with books on every floor. The first floor had a large room full of little boxes packed with cards (That was before computers). On the cards were the names of authors and the titles of books. We were expected to find the books we wanted without knowing which books we were looking for.

"How I wish my brother were here," I cried quietly to myself. "He would be able to find the books and do the reports easily."

I did not dare ask anyone how to find the books I needed. They might see my Dumb-Dumb T-shirt. Somehow I managed to find something and write some words in a folder that looked like a research paper. I honestly do not remember how I was able to get through that first year with decent grades. I know I never went back to the library. It was too intimidating.

The Big Treehouse

As the end of the second term drew near some of my friends began to talk about the military service. "They give you some tests to find out what you would be good at," I overheard them say, "and then they train you in that field and give you a job."

That sounded good to me. Surely Uncle Sam would be able to find a place where I would fit in. With their training program I would learn how to do something useful. I had also heard that their token master never cut anyone off from the land of the living unless they did something really bad. I did not expect to get many promotions, but I knew I was not bad – just dumb. I joined the Air Force and became part of one of the safest treehouses in the jungle.

After a couple of weeks of basic training at Lackland Air Force Base we were given a battery of tests. While waiting for the results I was having nightmares about spending the rest of my life peeling potatoes for the successful airmen who were allowed to go on to exciting careers. I would be left behind, all alone and exposed.

When they posted the results I was sure there must be a mistake. They were going to ship me off to electronics school at Keesler Air Force Base in Biloxi, Mississippi. I could not even do basic arithmetic. I had bluffed my way through High School but I knew this would be different. My T-shirt was about to be exposed again and there was nothing I could do about it. If I went on to Keesler it would soon become evident how dumb I was. If I called attention to the mistake I would also be exposed.

In about two weeks I found myself in a military classroom studying electronics. I was already sewing together a "Hero" jacket as an electronics technician. I could not believe it. "A Dumb-Dumb in electronics school, I thought. "What is the U.S.A.F. coming to?"

The continual yelling of the sergeant kept me from retreating into my imagination closet. I was not sure what they would do to me if they caught me drawing in my closet. So I studied. I did not know what else to do. The excitement of learning how those mysterious radar sets worked also helped keep me in the outside world. The joy of learning the "how" and "why" returned.

They posted reports of our progress after several weeks in the classroom. Much to my amazement according to their records I was doing very well. I was actually doing better than 90% of the other fellows who were with me in the class.

"How can this be," I asked myself. "How can a Dumb-Dumb do well in electronics school?" I assumed there must be a mistake in the records or this must be an exceptionally dumb class. Of course I told no one of my doubts. I acted as though I expected to do well. I had discovered a new way to cover my T-shirt. I pretended to be smart. *The Great Pretender* became my theme song.

On the Beach

Our first break came and I had gone to the beach just outside Biloxi, Mississippi. The question of identity was oozing its way to the surface. Something very real seemed to be emerging but I had no idea what to do with it.

"Could it be that I am not really dumb?" That possibility almost swept me off my feet. But there was something peaceful about the movement of the sand beneath the surface of the incoming tide. "I might have a place in this jungle after all." I mulled that over as the waves moved more sand from under my feet.

The pleasant thoughts continued to flow in with the waves. I am not sure how long I lingered there in the surf. It was as though time had been suspended at high tide. There was no movement, only the sense of being there. I was simply present to life. I was a person.

The tide began to shift. The breeze was increasing and I suddenly became aware that it was getting late. It was time for me to return to the base. I felt the sand shifting under my feet as a thousand little particles scampered, like my thoughts, back into hiding—back into the security of the deep—as though they were frightened by emerging consciousness.

The air began to chill and I suddenly realized I was walking on the beach with my T-shirt exposed. The thought that I might not actually be dumb threatened me to the core. I had become so identified with my T-shirt that I thought it was the real me. It was as though I might even cease to be a person if I admitted I was smart.

"Who do you think you are?" The accusing voice of my internalized father came from my closet. "Your Dumb-Dumb credentials have been stamped and verified in every stage of your life. You are dumb and you know it. Come back to reality."

So I came back to reality. Or did I just come out of reality back into my make-believe world? Which was real? Was it the beach or was it the base? How could I know? At any rate the spell had been broken and I could not continue to pursue the matter anyway. I had to get back to the base and face the exposure that I felt would certainly come.

I was inwardly puzzled for several weeks as the sense of 'becoming' remained. As the reality of the experience drifted back into the sea of unconsciousness I finally concluded I must be the sort of Dumb-Dumb who is clever enough to bluff the teachers into thinking I knew more than I really did. All my teachers had tried to tell me I was smarter than I thought I was. I had been able to fool all of them.

The more I thought about it the more it began to make sense. Somehow the cover-up techniques I had developed were so effective that no one knew how dumb

I was – except me. I was actually able to convince people I could understand things no dumb-dumb could possibly understand.

"Now that is an ability that could prove to be useful in the jungle," I thought. But when I considered it more seriously I knew I would not be able to do that consistently. Eventually I would get caught. The fear of exposure returned.

"Probably I've just had some lucky breaks." I heard myself speaking almost audibly. "All that thinking on the beach was nothing more than tension vaporizing into wishful imaginations."

Graduation day finally came at Keesler. We were all awarded our certificates and assigned to various places in the world. My assignment was near Tokyo, Japan. I had heard about that place. One could buy cameras and watches, even tailored suits for almost nothing. (That was before inflation came to Japan.)

"Here's my chance to collect some tokens of acceptability without paying a lot of money," I dreamed. "I can show off all my stuff when I return to the States. People will think I am successful."

I put on my neon "Electronics-Hero" jacket, boarded the airplane and off I went "into the wild blue yonder."

"Me, an electronics technician!" Boy was I excited.

The Mantle of Mediocrity

The experience of my first few weeks in Japan was a real letdown. My assignment was to Yokota Air Force Base, but I had to stay in a transit barrack in Yokohama until the official orders caught up with me. The crew I had been assigned to did not know I was coming. So I waited. I secretly suspected the Air Force had discovered their mistake. There was nothing I could do about it and I was not allowed off base so I could not run away.

I did not have a friend within six thousand miles. I was alone, and I was lonely.

I smoked over two packs of cigarettes a day during that time. It did not help but at least it kept me occupied. Everyone else was coming in one day and leaving the next. No one was even interested in a game of cards. The worst thing of all was that no one noticed my neon "Hero" jacket. They were all too busy polishing their own badges.

The orders finally arrived and they took me to Yokota Air Force Base. But when I reported for duty another problem surfaced. Since my work would be in an area where Top Secret information was available I would need a security clearance. They assigned me to a little shop that repaired broken radar equipment while I waited.

Most of the radar units they asked me to work on looked like they had been built in the Stone Age – out of stone. I had not seen anything like that during my training. The old "how-and-why" syndrome returned with a new dimension. Not only did I want to know how and why, I also needed to know what the unit was supposed to do when I finished with it.

I felt as though one of the buttons of my "Hero" shirt had dropped off. Just as my T-shirt was about to be exposed one of the airmen working there took me aside and explained the rules of the Air Force game.

"The rules are simple," he said. "If anyone does his work too well it makes the rest of the group look bad. As a penalty for doing exceptional work *your nose will turn brown.* The sentence is exclusion from the land of the living. You become a marked man and will be shunned by those in the venerated community of the complacent."

To be part of the "in group" was important to me and I certainly did not want my nose to turn brown. Like an *ovum* I received that deceptive *word-seed*, relaxed, sewed the button back on my jacket and went back to work. This was comfortable. I could work slowly, think carefully about the hows and whys and even make a few mistakes. If I did something dumb I could simply refer to the brown-nose rule that would not allow me to do well.

I got myself a new shirt, sewed on the word "Inconspicuous" and, with my mantle of mediocrity, joined the ranks of the complacent.

The security clearance came through and I settled into my new position in the Big Treehouse. Uncle Sam was becoming a security symbol for me. I could look to him and know he would take care of me even if I did a few dumb things. I knew what was expected of me and I knew how to do it. Most of all I felt free to make mistakes. People would think I was only keeping my nose clean.

The Effect of Received Words: The Power of Sheol

The word that my dad had spoken over me had convinced me I was dumb. It had never been a fully conscious thought but its influence governed my attitude and my behavior. I had learned to fear rejection and to order my behavior so as to be accepted, even if only superficially.

If I had been aggressive and selected the "Success" crowd as "my people" the situation would have been different. I would have been willing to face the "brown-nose" accusations in order to be accepted in the community of the successful. In either case the dynamic behind the behavior would have been a striving for acceptance and fear of rejection.

Regardless of how we deal with the negative, deceptive words spoken over us, if we allow them to define who we are they will have power over us. The fear of separation continues to creep in with its death trap. The power of Sheol is subtle in its deception. Driven to act in a specific way to avoid separation we end up with only superficial relationships. *Superficial relationships are only another form of separation.* We have only tokens of acceptance, not real intimacy.

We are not merely separated from others when we pretend; we are separated from our true selves as well. The cover-up behavior we choose becomes a wall between ourselves and others Psychologists call them defense mechanisms. The self we present to others is alienated from the self that is hiding behind the protective wall. Since we seldom let anyone inside our wall we live isolated lives. *Intimacy is impossible from the other side of a wall.*

But there are those who are driven to gain acceptance in the next higher group. No matter how successful one becomes there is always someone somewhere who is doing better so the marker for success moves away from the present level to the next level up. Since there is still a feeling of being unsuccessful they increase their efforts to be accepted as part of the next level.

In either case, whether driven to remain on the lower level or driven to climb, the efforts are attempts to gain acceptance. Relationships based on having, doing and achieving can never develop into intimate relationships.

Even those who choose to be in the ranks of the complacent cannot remain in that condition very long. Sooner or later the drive to become what we were created to be returns with its striving. Few are willing to wander in the wilderness of non-achievement for long unless they have lost the vigor of youth. Here the power of Sheol is experienced as depression.

While the comfort of complacency does provide a measure of rest, the deep desire to flourish will increase until movement returns. If that movement is motivated by feelings of worthlessness the movement will be a striving for acceptance either from peers or from the next higher group. This back and forth movement continues as long as there is a vestige of caring about oneself and one's relationships.

There are businessmen, for example, who are unable to relax and be with their families because they are striving to rise to the next higher income bracket. Upward mobility is the measure of personal worth. The extra money is not the real motivating factor. They want recognition and acceptance within a group they consider to be one step higher. The problem is exposed when they gain that recognition and still strive to move upward. There is always a higher plateau.

We are always in limbo between where we have been and where we want to go. It is like being on the threshold between two rooms; we are not in either place. We are not a part of either group. Even though I was complacent I was not connected to the others in the group because I wanted to be elsewhere. Not one of us is really content to be less than what we can be. Here again the issue is not what we accomplish but what we are becoming.

The writer of Ecclesiastes saw this: "Then I saw that all labor and all skill in work come from a man's envy of his neighbor. This also is vanity and striving after wind," (Ecclesiastes, 4:4).

Many are not able to stop pressing long enough to ask why. They secretly know the answer but it is too painful to consider the possibility that, apart from productivity and possessions, they may have no value as a person, no right to belong anywhere. Some may even begin to think they have no right to be alive.

Those who strive often hide behind high-sounding clichés: "If a job is worth doing, it's worth doing well." That is true enough. The question we are raising here is whether one is working toward improvement and a job well done or is struggling to produce external evidence of his acceptability as a person? Our struggle exposes the fact that we do not really believe we are worth it. *If we are not at home within ourselves we will never be at home in the good times or in the struggles of life.*

If we are really working for the sake of our families would we not want to have those extra hours with them rather than in the marketplace? Families require time and energy. If we spend more time and energy than necessary apart from them, we deprive them of our presence and the input they need from us. We are only using them as an excuse for our drivenness.

We are striving after wind. It is painful to become aware that we are driven by a dynamic within ourselves over which we have little control. We feel as though we are caught on some sort of carousel that will not stop for us to get off. Life has aptly been called a rat race. We run over each other or ignore each other as we chase after our own piece of cheese. This is the power of Sheol in operation and it is a bondage through fear of death.

When we long to belong we give evidence that we do not feel like we do belong. We do not long for what we know we have. So our striving is evidence that we doubt that we have a right to belong without productivity or possessions. It is just as true, though less obvious, when our striving takes the form of under-achievement. In this case we are trying to be accepted by the ranks of the complacent. This is also the power of Sheol.

There are deeper questions most people never allow to surface, "Would anyone accept me if they knew what I am hiding? Can anyone love me just for me, without any performance, position or possessions?" When these questions are allowed to rise up they bring with them a new and unexpected dynamic. We begin to do things (perhaps unconsciously) to expose what we consider to be the real self.

We see two kinds of behavior patterns here. Chapter two had a diagram distinguishing between what we "*are*" and what we "*think*" we are. We see the two behavior patterns issuing from the imagined self (see Fig. #2). On the left there is behavior intended to cover up the poor self-image. These are the things we do and say to avoid exposing our T-shirts.

On the right is the behavior designed to expose the T-shirt, though it is usually unconscious. The purpose of this behavior is to discover if anyone loves us in spite of how "dumb" we are. We are only aware that we do dumb things for no apparent reason. We step back and ask ourselves, "Why did I do a dumb thing like that?" Or we give an equally lame excuse for our behavior. We should not be surprised when others reject us. We have already rejected our true selves.

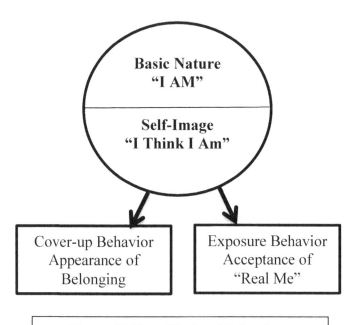

Figure #2 Two Kinds of Behavior

Later we will discuss a third kind of behavior which we will call "expression" behavior. We now raise the more significant question: "Is there a way out? Is there any possibility of coming to a place where we can be the kind of person with the freedom to express the reality of who we are with no fear of embarrassment or rejection?"

Cover-up produces deceptive acceptance because there is no real intimacy when we cover our real self. But exposure produces obvious rejection and isolation. People shun those who dare to reveal their undershirts. This is a real dilemma, a real catch 22. You lose the possibility of intimacy either way.

Is there an alternative? Is there a way to reveal your true self with no fear of being left out? Is there a way out from under the power of Sheol?

We turn our attention to this question in the next chapter.

Five: VENETIAN BLINDS

Light Brooding over the Deep

I remember well those days in Japan. After working through the frustration of the first few weeks I became very comfortable in my position. My responsibilities were clearly defined and I enjoyed what I was doing. I even considered a permanent career in the Air Force. My superiors were satisfied with my work and encouraged me regularly. I was up for a promotion. Everything seemed right except I was uneasy about something I was not able to define.

The internal turbulence came to the surface when a sergeant came to invite me to go to church with him. At that time the military made the religious preferences available to the various church groups on base. The sergeant was a member of the same denomination I had grown up in. Because of my religious training I felt I *ought* to go so I agreed. But when Sunday came I didn't want to go. I stayed in the barrack.

"What has church ever done for me?" I thought. "All they ever do is sing the same old songs, pray the same old prayers and listen to the same old sermons." I did not notice that my attention was focused only on what *they* were doing or not doing. That helped me ignore what I was doing.

I had a Bible but never read it for two reasons. First, I didn't enjoy reading anything – it reminded me of libraries. (I learned later that my reading problem was due to dyslexia.) Secondly, I knew if I read the Bible it would remind me of all the things I was doing wrong. I wanted to be part of the crowd that was having a good time.

As I look back I realize I was not really having a good time. No one else was either. *None of us ever stopped having fun long enough to notice we were not having fun.* We were busy pretending to enjoy our diversions. The distractions helped us ignore our conscience.

Most of the time I tried to stay out of my imagination closet as well. The quiet closet of meditation and secret adventures was no longer quiet and it was no longer exciting. When I went in I was only reminded of the "oughts" and "ought-nots" that I was not trying to live by. *My closet had become a place of condemnation* rather than a place of rest and peace. I could not even receive imaginary acceptance by retreating.

At eight years of age I made a commitment to Jesus. That was 1945. An evangelist had come to our church in Carlsbad, New Mexico and preached for a week. His sermon on "Running the Race" caught my attention. I can still remember the large chart he had drawn on a white bed-sheet and displayed before the congregation. (That was before overhead projectors!) It was a picture of an arena with a race track. A variety of runners were illustrated at different points on the track of life. At the end of the race was a crown for those who finished well.

His illustrations captured my boyhood imagination. The *word-seed* was planted in the *ovum* of my heart and it was germinating as he spoke. In my childhood devotion I wanted to run this race and I wanted to run it well.

"To begin the race," the preacher said, "you must be baptized." Then he read some Bible verses.

I went forward that night and received immersion in

water. I can still remember the congregation singing "*Just as I am*," as I went down the aisle, and "*All to Jesus I Surrender*," as I came up out of the water. Even at that time I knew something real had happened. They said I had become a new creature. I had no idea what that meant. I only knew that there was peace deep inside the closet of my imagination.

In Japan my closet had long since become cluttered with many voices clambering for attention. I had forgotten the inner stillness that came that night as I responded to the preacher's invitation. That night I was at peace on a very deep level. In Japan I was too busy finding out what the world had to offer. The light of that new life that was in me was clouded and diminished by guilt and shame.

The sergeant continued to come by and ask why I was not coming to church. I continued to make excuses. His visits reminded me of the contrast between what I knew to be right and what I was doing. *The inner conflict was like the pressure of a baby's head against the cervix.* It returned more forcefully with each visit of the sergeant.

"Maybe I should try to quit smoking before I start going back to church again," I thought to myself. "Then I would feel like I belong there."

I honestly tried to quit several times. Once I was successful for almost two weeks. I made a card to remind me I was quitting. To provide adequate motivation I drew a stairway on the card with "heaven" written at the top and "hell" written on the bottom.

"Each cigarette I smoke will be a step downward," I reminded myself. I placed the card in my pocket to replace the cancer sticks. It did not occur to me at that time that I had not provided a way to take steps upward.

That card worked well until a friend offered me a drag. I accepted it. There I was on my way down. I was not really surprised. I suppose I really expected to fail. For a short time I was faithful to keep a record of my smokes on the card. When it became obvious what was happening I did the only sensible thing; I threw away the card and looked for more exciting diversions.

One of my favorite distractions was riding my motorcycle out into the Japanese countryside. I had learned enough Japanese to relate to the people. I visited many places where very few Americans ever went. These excursions took me to ancient shrines and points of historical and cultural interest. The country was beautiful and the people were kind and hospitable. But I was running away from myself.

At times I felt as though I was looking for something I had lost or misplaced, or maybe never had. "The time on the beach in Biloxi, Mississippi seemed so real," I thought. "If only I could recapture that timeless moment and continue my search for my true identity." But those moments cannot be created; they come and go as they please.

At other times I seemed to be running away from something. I certainly did not want to face the reality of "Dumb-Dumb" in my present lifestyle. I had myself well covered from the view of others. Many were probably envious of the freedom I appeared to have. But I knew what was on the inside. At least I thought I knew. I was afraid to look too closely. It might be worse than I imagined. So I continued to look at the countryside . . . anywhere outside myself.

The Other Side of Stillness

The moment of reality came one morning after I had been on duty as night watchman. The night shift had not been difficult and I had rested well. I had left the venetian blinds open when I went to bed that night. As I awoke the bright sun filled the room with light and painted a black and white stripped pattern on the wall opposite my bunk. Its radiance brought the promise of a good day. And so it was to be.

The Air Force Base had barracks that were divided by a hallway with semi-private sleeping quarters on either side. Each room had from two to six bunks with adequate locker space and a desk. I was one of the fortunate airmen who shared a room with only one other person. For all practical purposes I had the room alone because my roommate was always out with the boys.

I was allowed to post a "Day Sleeper" sign on my door because of guard duty the night before. Unlike some other barracks that sign was respected in our area. With my roommate on a three day pass I felt safe. I was alone, much like I had been on the beach in Biloxi, Mississippi. The identity questions were beginning to rise to the surface again. I was alone. This time I was lonely.

"What am I becoming?" The question greeted me as my eyelids lifted to receive the morning light. The question was not as pleasant as it had been before.

I dressed and sat at the reading desk. Looking out through the venetian blinds I saw children gathering for their swimming lessons at the pool across the street. They were running, jumping, and laughing freely. Life seemed so simple for them.

"If only I could be like a little child again," I sighed. But I knew one can never go back. I wondered if it would really be desirable to be a child again anyway. What possible advantage could there be in that? I would only have to grow up again with no guarantee that things would be any better the second time around.

The swimming instructor arrived. The sound of children's laughter frittered away into the dressing rooms. I lit a cigarette and waited, though I did not know what I was waiting for. If anyone had asked I probably would have been startled by the question. I was waiting but did not know I was waiting. I was just staring into space.

The silent stillness returned. "Perhaps I'll take a ride on my motorcycle," I reflected. "It's a nice day for that sort of thing."

That was a pleasant, inviting thought but the silence immediately apprehended me. There would be no diversions or distractions that day. Something—or someone—was calling, wooing from the other side of stillness. I did not know what was happening. Even if I had known the Lord was approaching I would not have known what to do. I would have run away. I did not yet know about his loving kindness. I had only heard of his anger and condemnation.

The thought of his coming would not have occurred to me anyway. My religious background was suspicious of people who claimed to have encounters with God. We thought they were either deceived or candidates for the Funny Farm. Nothing in my upbringing or training had prepared me to anticipate or even to expect what was coming to me from the *other side of this silence*. But I was captive to the moment and could only wait.

I left the cigarette in the ash tray and went to check the door. It was locked. I needed to know that for some reason. As I returned to the smoke rising from the cigarette I thought, "I do not need that right now." I doused it in the ash tray and reclined on my bunk. Folding my hands on my chest I stared back and forth, up at the ceiling and over to the pattern of light and dark from the sun beaming through the venetian blinds.

The light and shadow pattern on the wall was a harbinger. My thoughts were racing back and forth through the various experiences of the past few months. Some were light and delightful; some were dark and dismal. I did not know what to do. I could not withdraw from dawning reality and I could not go forward. I was hostage to the impending event. I had to wait for "IT" to approach me, so I lingered there in the stillness.

Suddenly I was aware that Someone was in the room with me. He had not come in; He was just there. I did not see Him but his Presence filled the room. The Presence was so real that I lifted my hands to receive His embrace. I knew it was the Lord. I do not know how I knew; I just knew. I knew He loved me and accepted me as I was, even though He knew all about my present lifestyle. ***The room was filled with Liquid Love and I drank deeply.***

I had been immersed in water as a child. Now I was being immersed in His love. For the first time in my life I knew I was loved. "*Jesus Loves Me, This I Know*." Before this experience I believed what the Bible said about His love. Like Job I had heard of Him by the hearing of the ear, but now the eyes of my heart beheld Him (Job. 32:5). My *heart* received his love. The experience contained a word-seed. *Receiving love is*

64

deeper than merely believing a doctrine of God's love.

None of my fantasies in the closet had ever been like this. This was real. I was fully aware of the natural surroundings in the room, but His presence was far more real than any of that. I had come face to face with another reality beyond anything we normally call real. How can I say it*? It was real reality! Although it took place in the closet it was not imaginary.*

It was as though the one who lives on the other side of the closet had rent a veil, received me to Himself beyond the vail and embraced me as a newborn baby. This I know; He was there and he loved me with an everlasting, unconditional love. *I was in the bosom of the Mother heart of Father God.* He embraced me even with all the shadows I knew were there inside me.

Something within me had come of age. The seed that was planted within me as a boy was breaking through the soil and reaching for the light – and beyond. The "me" inside was very much alive. The life in me was quickened by the realization and acknowledgement that the "Beloved of heaven" had received me into His arms. He knew my fears and my failures, the light and the shadows. He knew what I was hiding from others and from myself. He loved me anyway. He loved me as I was.

I was NOT alone and I was NOT lonely*.* As I lay there looking up at my raised hands I thought how dumb this would look if someone saw me. But I knew it was not dumb. Being received into the bosom of the Mother heart of Father God had dispelled the fear of rejection. (Both masculinity and femininity are in God.) Everything was so right. It was okay. It was more than okay. It was delightfully real and true.

Lowering my hands to my chest again I continued to drink of his presence. With each inhaling breath I was receiving love, joy and peace. With each exhaling breath I was being relieved of insecurity, unworthiness and inadequacy. His loving presence was washing away feelings of guilt and defilement – like a river overflowing its bank and bringing moisture and nutrients to the soil.

Later I wrote these words:

> Then there was evening,
> Then there was morning,
>> When silent streams of sunlight,
>>> Seeping through the window shades
>>>> To greet emerging consciousness,
> Have put to flight the savage shadows of the
>> Cloven Hoof;
> Then breaks Eternal Day.

The *sense* of His presence slowly faded but His presence remained. From that day to this I have known He is real. I knew then He would always there with His love. There was a residue remaining deep within. This presence would take me into experiences and accomplishments I had never dreamed possible for me. I spent the rest of the day enjoying this newness of life.

During the next few weeks there were visible signs of the freedom I was experiencing. The following Sunday I was in church but not because I felt obligated; I wanted to be there. There were also the cigarettes. One day I suddenly realized my roommate had smoked all the ones I left on the desk. *My desire for nicotine had gone up in smoke*. I had not decided to quit; it just happened. His love had set me free from a nasty habit even without my asking.

The Old Man and the New Man

That which came of age in me was not a product of the seed of the first Adam (mere humanity). The false human nature has nothing in itself to produce this deep change. Our false nature might conquer external activity (like smoking) but the change we speak of here is much deeper. *The false self that needs improvement is not up to the task of improving.* Any do-it-yourself kit for self-improvement is like an ovum trying to fertilize itself. The emerging of the new man in Christ, the "second Adam," (I Corinthians 15:47) is not simply an improved version of the old man. A radical change takes place in this transition. Some adjustments and additions to our diagram will help us explain this difference (see Fig. #3).

Jesus said to Nicodemus, "That which is born of flesh is flesh, and that which is born of Spirit is spirit. Do not marvel that I said to you, 'You must be born again'" (John 3:6-7).

Paul exhorted the Ephesians to "come out from the false self, which belongs to your former manner of life and is corrupt through deceitful desires, to be renewed in the spirit of your minds and sink into the true self, created after the likeness of God in true righteousness and holiness" (Ephesians 4:22-24).

As the false man is related to the seed of Adamic generation and corrupted through false words, so the true man is related to the seed of divine regeneration. As the old man is a product of the flesh, so the new man is a

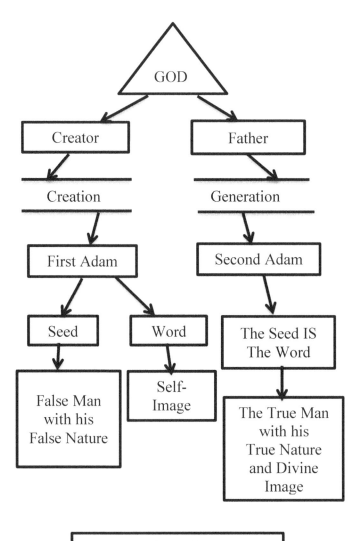

Figure # 3
Two Kinds of Generation

68

product of the Spirit. "Just as we have borne the image of the [false] man of dust, we shall also bear the image of the [true] man of heaven" (I Corinthians 15:49).

At the top of our diagram notice that Adam is a son of God by *creation* (Luke 3:38) and Christ is the Son of God by *generation*. Discussions about being born again must make clear the distinction between creation and generation. One does not impart his nature to something he builds in the same way he does when he begets a son or a daughter. A building will never participate in human nature even if it reflects the personality of the architect.

Man-as-man, as born of the seed of Adam and raised in falsehood, will never become God – he is a created being. Christ Jesus is the eternal Son of the eternal Father. He is the begotten Son who bears the image we humans were created to bear. "He is the radiance of the glory of God" (Hebrews 1:3) and "in him all the fullness of God was pleased to dwell" (Colossians 1:19).

As the begotten Son He has two things that interest us here. As the Word of God He has the divine nature of the Father, and He has within His spiritual "loins" the word-seed that can reproduce itself. *This seed impregnates the ovum of the human spirit and makes it possible for us to reflect the image of God that we were created to bear.*

In John chapter 3 Nicodemus missed the point of two key words in Jesus' statement, "You must be born again." Each of the two Greek words has a double meaning. The word **born** can also be translated "**begotten**," and the word **again** can also be translated "**from above**." The first reflects the difference between **motherhood** (born) and **fatherhood** (begotten). The second reflects the difference between **repetition** (again) and **source** (from above). Nicodemus asked, "Can a man enter a **second time** (repetition) into his mother's womb (motherhood) and **be born**?" Nicodemus misunderstood both words.

The fatherhood of God is one of the major themes in John's Gospel. One's nature is determined by the seed. Seed comes from the sire. Pig seed produces pig nature and human seed produces human nature. The mother's womb contains the ovum and is the environment in which the seed has opportunity to grow and develop. That environment may influence the development, but if the seed is from a pig the offspring will be a pig. If the seed is from a man the offspring will be human.

Concerning the question of repetition, what possible advantage could there be in repeating the birth experience? Even if it were possible the pig would still be a pig and the human would still be a human. Our point is this: Flesh (a human "doing" apart from God) will manifest more flesh. If we could "go through that again" some things might be different but nothing fundamental will have changed. We would still be without a living relationship with God. Even if we were able to train a pig to eat with a knife and fork it would still be a pig.

We tend to limit the idea of fatherhood and sonship in the Gospel of John to the relationship between Jesus and his Father. Yet John's message is clear; "But to all who received him, who believed in his name, he gave the right and ability to become children of God, who were begotten, not of blood nor of the will of the flesh nor of the will of man, but of God," (John 1:12-13). To be begotten of God is clearly to be begotten from above.

Peter reminded us that "he has caused us to be born

again to a living hope through the resurrection of Jesus Christ from the dead" (I Peter 1:3). Peter used a term that means again in the sense of a second time but he gave precise definition to this when he added, "You have been born again, not of perishable seed but of imperishable, through the living and abiding word of God," (I Peter 1:23). This second time is fundamentally different from the first time. The seed of this generation comes from God; it comes from above. We are begotten from above.

In answer to Nicodemus' question, then, it is indeed impossible for a man to enter the mother's womb a second time. It is not only impossible; it would accomplish nothing. The birth of which Jesus spoke can never result from man's will or man's efforts. Man as producer can never manifest Spirit as his product. Flesh is flesh and can only manifest flesh. Man can never be born of the Spirit by a work of the flesh; he can only receive it like an ovum receives seed, as an act of the heavenly Father, as a miracle from above.

Having received the miracle of new birth we do not immediately become spiritual giants. We do not come into the family of God as mature sons. As we grow up physically so also we must grow up spiritually. As there are struggles in our physical and emotional development, so there are struggles in our spiritual development. As we face the struggles by the Spirit we grow in our ability to manifest true sonship (Romans 8:17-19).

Many people in their desire to manifest the abundant life are depending on their false nature to produce a spiritual reality. One may be able to manifest tokens of wealth by human efforts but that wealth never satisfies the longing for more. We may be satisfied for a time, but when the new wears off we long for more of what we believe will fulfill us. Money often makes life easier in many respects, but ease of life is not our goal here. Someone asked Henry Ford, "How much money is enough?" His response was, "Just a little bit more."

I recently heard of a man who had "manifested" several billion dollars. He claims to be living a fulfilled life of satisfaction. He is a very generous man and gives much to charities. It is reported that he has a desire to be the world's first trillionaire. I asked myself, "If he is as satisfied as he says he is, why does he want more? Why is he working so hard to manifest more?"

Manifesting more stuff will never bring you into wholeness. Stuff is available to those who experience abundant life but it is not the focus. The new life we desire is only available to the new *true-person* who is no longer identified by his background, possessions or profession. The abundant life is available to those who receive the divine life of "Christ in you the hope of glory," (Colossians 1:27). Those who have been born of the Word of God actually have the life of God living within them. It takes spiritual discipline to "put off the false [old]" and "put on the true [new]," *but the new is in there.*

The training necessary to manifest the life of Christ, the truly divine life, began even while I was in Japan but it continued for many years as I returned to receive an education and to pursue the call and commission I had received in the barrack of Yokota Air Force Base. That training is continuing even to this day.

As this book approaches publication I am approaching my 80th birthday. Today I can say with Paul, "It is no longer I who live, but Christ who lives in me,"

(Galatians 2:20). This is not something I have that sets me apart from others. We are all created in the image of God and his life is potentially in all of us. When we allow Christ to live out his life in us we are only becoming what we were created to become. That "becoming" is a *potential* for all who are created in His image – to all humans. What I am suggesting is that the human spirit is like an ovum. Apart from the divine seed being implanted, one will not be able to manifest the divine life.

Because we are raised in a culture that fails to reflect the divine life—a culture that is focused on the external and on the self—we are in need of training to overcome our false images of reality. That training is not only in classroom settings. Much too often the classroom is the place where false concepts are presented. Life itself is a training ground. Experiences—both good and bad—are opportunities to learn how to live an abundant life.

There is a specific training necessary for each individual person. We each need training designed to prepare us for the particular part we are designed to play in the community. We need training for the contribution we are designed to make. But in the process of formal training we often get caught up in a way of thinking that is counterproductive. While we are learning how to do what we are designed to do we often get side-tracked. But the detour can also teach us if we are willing to learn.

My training is the topic of the next chapter. This is my story. But every person's story follows a similar path even though each path will have different emphases and different goals. Mine was in a college classroom as a student and as a professor. Yours may be in the business world or on a farm. The patterns are the same.

Six: OVERCOATS AND ARMORS

My experience of Father's love in Japan completely redirected my life. My desire to make the USAF a permanent career was no longer there. I began working with a local missionary and even preached a time or two. I knew I would never be satisfied doing anything other than teaching people about the love of God. It was more than a question of personal satisfaction; there was a sense of the destiny of a divine calling. I knew I must prepare myself to teach.

When I returned to the States and was discharged from the military I got a job in Albuquerque, New Mexico because I did not want to be in the town where my dad was. But he died in a car accident a few months later, so I moved back home to be with my mother for a time. We lived only about sixty-five miles south of Portales, NM where there was a university that had a Religious Studies program. With a sense of confidence beyond my earlier freshman experience in Albuquerque I enrolled in Eastern New Mexico University the following fall and begin a totally new journey.

I chose that university for several reasons. It had a Department of Religion funded by various churches. As a child my religious training carried warnings about the "destructive doctrines" of other denominations and seminaries. The head of the Department of Religion at ENMU was a member of the church I grew up in so I felt safe. The second reason was that tuition was very reasonable compared to seminaries and private schools. A third reason was that it was close to home.

Disillusionment

My concept of a religious education was limited at that time. Somehow I thought the instructors would tell me where all the Bible verses were that proved how right we were. All the preachers I grew up listening to assured us we were the only ones with pure doctrine. All I had to do was memorize all the proof-texts and learn how to string the verses together into sermons. I was in for some real big surprises.

I did relatively well that first year in spite of the trauma of discovering how small my vision of reality was. The more I learned about the historical and cultural background of the Bible the more I became aware of my ignorance. As I learned Greek it became clear that some of the doctrines of our church denomination were a result of straining out gnats and swallowing camels.

Many of our favorite arguments were nothing more than *trying to force the text to say what we wanted to hear rather than allowing the text to speak for itself.* Most of the questions we were asking of the text had nothing to do with the message the author was trying to convey. This was the beginning of my disillusionment. A new age was dawning for me.

I was still naïve enough to believe that the people in our denomination would be excited to learn the things I was learning. Since their motto was "If the Bible says it we believe it," they would certainly be interested in learning what those Bible verses "really" meant; at least that is what I thought. Why should they not be happy for me to tell them how wrong they have been? It is a good thing I did not have to face disillusionment until later.

Two dynamics began to operate in my life as I continued to learn. *The first dynamic* was a deep desire to know and understand what was real and true. Much of what I believed before entering college was either misleading or contrary to the facts. Each new thing I learned exposed another area where I had been indoctrinated.

Making a break from the futile ways inherited from our spiritual fathers (I Peter 1:18) is a difficult and threatening process but it is necessary if we want to manifest reality in our lives. My confidence in human authority began to fade. I must discover truth for myself. Too many have *borrowed truths* which they have never questioned. It is only by personal *experience* of truth that it becomes real in a person's life. I wanted to experience the depths of God and of His Word. Merely quoting what others have said never fed my spirit.

The Pitfall of Intellectual Pursuit

Little did I know that the task I had selected for myself would swell up like a tsunami tidal wave and overwhelm me. Each time I tried to establish certainty on any given issue I would come face-to-face with several other areas of uncertainty. Each new door in the University only led to another hallway with several new doors each leading to other hallways and other doors. There was very little substance behind any of those doors. There were only more questions.

I was lost in the labyrinth of academic pursuit. My heart was lifted up and my eyes were raised too high (cf. Psalm 131:1). The task I had selected was too big for me.

I began to look for something, or someone, from which I could derive some sense of direction. I read philosophers and psychologists even though that was not part of the degree plan. This was a personal quest. I just had to know. I read theologians, philosophers, psychologists and scholars of world religions. I felt there must be some hidden ingredient I had overlooked. I came to identify with the Preacher in the book of Ecclesiastes, "…in much wisdom is much vexation, and he who increases knowledge increases sorrow," (Ecclesiastes 1:18).

What I had not known before I started this journey was that once you have begun the journey there is no turning back short of insanity. There is no guarantee that the road will lead to a happy ending. During the difficult years I penned this meditation:

Now I Must Know

Looking for guidance
From one who has gone before.
Someone is there in the fog.

"Can you help a man lost on his way
And direct him which path he should take?"

"I'm here where I am,"
His reply was so pleasant,
"I see no farther ahead.
I have come this far from who knows whence,
From here the path leads who knows whither.
Perhaps I am lost as well."

Then came the whirlwind shifting the fog.
It covered him up, took him away,
Or perhaps uncovered a path.
There's one way to know!

Where I've been there was nothing to keep,
Where I am there is nothing to take,
So now I must go,
For now I must know,
Now I must know,
I must know,
Must know.

I had indeed reached the age of seeking but I found nothing. The training I received taught me to look for answers in all the wrong places. The driving desire for more knowledge was beginning to control my life. Never again would I be content to wander in the wilderness of complacency. *I had been stung by the Asp of Eden.* I saw no alternative but to continue seeking after academic certainty. Seeking academic knowledge, even the knowledge of good, had become a smoke screen blocking my view of the One who had come to me in Japan.

I actually thought the way to know him was through the intellect. Having begun in the Spirit I was trying to advance by the flesh, (Galatians 3:3). Even if I had wanted to I would not have been able to return to the previous stage. One can never go back, not really. *The place where you were is no longer there because places change with time just as we do.*

The Prison of Comparison

This brings us to the *second dynamic* which began to operate in my life. It is related to the first. The more I learned the more I became aware of how much I did not know. I did something which I suppose many students do. I compared my level of understanding to that of the upper classmen and sometimes even to my professors. Naturally I came up short. It seemed they knew so much more. As I became more aware of how much there is to learn I compared their knowledge with my relative ignorance and felt inadequate.

The old "Dumb-Dumb" syndrome returned. It came back slowly and subtly and it came with the impulse to cover up once again. The fear of being exposed (the power of Sheol) grew quietly as I became the upper classman. I remember well the feeling that I did not measure up especially now that I was comparing myself with the graduate students and the scholars who wrote the commentaries. To maintain the 'upper classman' image I began to pretend to know more than I actually knew.

This developed so slowly that I did not recognize it for several years. I realize now that the *fear of exposure was greater than the desire for integrity*. Thus I began to weave the fabric of what was to become a three-piece suit to cover up my "Dumb-Dumb" T-shirt. I would write the word "Smart" on the front. It is necessary to wear a "Smart-Suit" when you are on a college campus. It is part of the social paradigm of university life.

The new confidence I received in Japan had become a fleeting confidence. The focus of my attention had shifted from the presence of God to my own ability to use big vocabulary words and complex philosophical constructs to convince others that I knew what I was talking about. I was as confused and insecure as any other student. I was too insecure even to face it myself and I was certainly unwilling to let anyone else see what I was hiding.

I can still remember the anxiety with which I approached the day of graduation. I had a high grade-point average and was a member of the honor society, but I was not personally convinced those honors were really mine. I knew how much I did not know. As though this were not enough to produce anxiety I heard stories of students who had received their folder at graduation with no diploma inside. I just knew that would happen to me. What would I tell my friends?

I even had visions of walking across the platform and watching with embarrassment as the Dean fumbled around looking for my folder. I could almost hear him saying, "I do not seem to have your folder here. Apparently my secretary failed to inform you that there is a mistake in our records. You have not yet completed all the requirements for graduation." I just knew the one course I lacked would be something I would not be able to complete.

The big day came. I donned the scholar's robe and walked to the platform with an air of confidence. The Dean called my name, handed me my folder and I walked off. I did not dare look inside the folder while others were watching. They might think I was insecure. Later I opened and looked inside. Sure enough there was a diploma inside. The amazing thing is that it had my name on it. I could not resist the thought, "What a dumb university! Imagine giving a degree to a "Dumb-Dumb."

Now it was legal for me to wear my "Smart-Suit" in public. I quickly began to parade my knowledge in Sunday schools and church services. I seldom thought of the experience in Japan any more. Without realizing it I had lost sight of the One who had approached me there. My attention was focused on knowledge gained by study. The search for certainty had robbed me of that fresh flow of life I had once known when I approached Scripture in His presence by the Spirit.

The perspective I grew up with was that the Holy Spirit had written the New Testament and then returned to heaven. God had given us a book and a mind. Our responsibility was to "work out your own salvation with fear and trembling," (Philippians 2:12). *I was trying and I was dying.* I never noticed the next verse, "for God is at work in you, both to will and to do for his good pleasure." Even if I had noticed I would not have understood anyway. I had forgotten (or never learned) how to listen to the Spirit while reading the Bible.

Occasionally I remembered the excitement of those days in Japan. A deep yearning would rise up within me as I wondered what had gone wrong. I longed to return to the simplicity of walking daily in his presence. Religious experiences had no place in the churches of my childhood training so I continued to concentrate on doctrine. As it was with the Pharisees, Bible knowledge had become a veil over my mind (II Corinthians 3:15).

Study kept me from facing the emptiness I felt. Those of us who were leaders in the churches were dry and hungry, but we covered it with religious jargon and kept ourselves distracted with church activities. As long as we used the right words and kept busy with church work we could at least convince others we were satisfied and fulfilled. We often even believed our own lie.

The light I had seen in Japan was eclipsed by academic training. I knew God was not dead, as some philosophers were saying, but I had become convinced that he was not available for personal fellowship apart from intense intellectual effort and strenuous religious activities on my part. The memory of his coming to me without my asking, without my knowing, and in the midst of my selfishness, now seemed more like a dream. I knew it was a real experience but I was not able to recapture the sense of his presence.

Unconsciously I had learned to rely on human wisdom to discern the meaning of the biblical text. Without recognizing it I was trying to proclaim "the testimony of God in lofty words of wisdom" rather than "in demonstration of the power of God" (I Corinthians 2:1-5). In those days I considered it a compliment when people said my teaching was over their heads. I never stopped to ask how I could legitimately call myself a teacher if no one understood what I was saying. People were impressed and entertained but there was no manifestation of divine life as there had been in Japan. I had forgotten that the "Dumb-Dumb" T-shirt was under the "Smart-Suit." I was totally unaware that I was covering something.

Having been programmed to look for God in the Bible using my mind, I assumed my need was for more intense study habits and a higher level of education. It did not occur to me that I had known him before I studied Greek and Church History. Driven to understand more deeply, and unconsciously obsessed with keeping my T-shirt hidden, I decided to continue my education. I saw no other option. So I enrolled in graduate school.

A Companion for the Journey

Meanwhile a young lady entered my life. I had been too insecure to pursue a relationship with girls but now that I was covered with "Smart-Suit" I felt more confident. Her name was Lynda Richards. She had been valedictorian of her High School class. *My "Smart-Suit" fell in love with her "Smart-Blouse."* She was deeply concerned for people and was always busy helping others instead of flirting as other girls did. That impressed me.

We joined hands and committed ourselves to one another for life. My "Smart-Suit" felt good about having a "Smart-Blouse" for a wife. As it turned out that is one of the smartest moves I have ever made. If I had seen her then for all she is I am sure I would have considered myself unworthy of such a treasure. But I was too focused on myself to look deeply at her. As most of you know, *no one takes off their cover-up on the honeymoon.* Sometimes the cover-up does not come off for many years. At least mine did not.

I finished the course work for the Master of Arts Degree shortly after we were married. My first teaching position was at The Victoria College in Victoria, Texas. The Bible Chair there was an arrangement where the church paid my salary and the school gave credit for the Bible courses I taught on campus. I became increasingly aware of my inadequacies. The students showed excitement over new insights they were receiving, but I felt insecure each time one would ask a question.

"What if I do not know the answer?" I would inwardly gasp. "My 'Smart-Suit' will fall open and my T-shirt will be exposed."

After two years of teaching I finally finished writing my thesis and received an M.A. degree from Eastern New Mexico University. I saw my graduate degree as a thick camel's hair overcoat with "Double-Smart" written on the front. I thought it would help me with my insecurities in the classroom. But the feelings actually intensified because now I was expected to know more. There would no longer be any excuse for not knowing the answers to questions from students.

Some students seemed to have an ability to sense which questions would threaten me most. Inevitably those questions would come up in class. When they did I simply made up answers with big words and high sounding phrases as I pulled my "Double-Smart" overcoat tightly around my neck. One more year of that was all I could handle. I had to continue my education, so I made plans to attend The University of Texas at Austin. I had to go for the "big one."

"I will get myself a Ph.D. in the Hebrew language from the Linguistics Department at The University of Texas," I thought. "No one will be able to see my T-shirt through that." I saw myself putting on metal armor, about an inch thick, with a helmet and a visor. Everything would be totally covered and it would not fall open when students asked difficult questions.

A more honorable motivation was under the surface just as it had been in undergraduate work. I thought I might be able to discover the element that was missing in my devotional life if I could just read the biblical text in the original languages. I was setting myself up for serious disillusionment because the intellect was never designed to find God. It is useful in talking to others about what you found, but all that talk is empty if the backdrop of intimacy with Father God is missing.

This turned out to be the most intensive study I had ever been involved in, but I expected that. After learning modern Israeli Hebrew we attended classes in which the professors taught in Hebrew; very little English was spoken. We studied every stage of the language from the ancient biblical text to the Mishnah, from Moshe Ben-Maimon (a Jewish philosopher of the Middle Ages) to Agnon (a modern Israeli poet). Then we took classes in the cognate languages: Aramaic, Arabic, Acadian and Ugaritic. I began to wear my armored vest long before I graduated. I was really impressed with myself. I was a Ph.D. candidate.

I still had a deep a hunger to touch reality as I had while in Japan, *once upon a time, in a land far away.* But I had come to believe the intensive study and seeking academic answers to religious and biblical questions would bring me closer to God. I was beginning to wonder whether He could be known at all. The experience in Japan was too real to deny. But every attempt to pursue Him intellectually only led to another blind alley. I knew He was there. I just did not know how to experience Him. I did not know to get "there" from "here."

The unequivocal knowledge of His existence drove me to continue my search. I was planning to begin work on a second Ph.D. as soon as I finished the one in Hebrew. I would have continued to pursue one degree after another if God had not intervened. After all there were other scholars who had more than one Ph.D. I was still comparing myself with the next level above me. I was reading from some scholars who had three or four PhDs. Had I continued in that vein my contribution to society would have been a series of articles in the academic journals that gather dust in the libraries and frighten the little dumb-dumbs who come to college to hide. I would have spent my life seeking answers to questions few people ever ask.

While finishing the final semester of the course work at Austin, I was planning my dissertation. My name was "accidentally" left off the list of those who received financial aid from the government for post-graduate studies. The Financial Aid office said they would try to work something out since they had made the mistake.

Then I received a letter from Eastern New Mexico University where I had been a student. They wanted me to return as an assistant professor. I accepted their invitation before I learned the grant came through and all my expenses would be paid to continue writing my dissertation. My Father God was leading me without my knowledge. He does not need me to understand.

The Implanted Word

I had come a long way since the Air Force days and I had learned many things on the journey. But nothing I had learned could compare with what was waiting for me in my new assignment. I had come through the age of seeking without finding and was about to enter the age of finding. I did not know that yet. I was just excited to get back to teaching. That was my joy, my gift and my calling. And I knew it.

One thing is apparent as I look back at those years of seeking and striving. The word implanted within the heart of a child has tremendous formative influence long after it is consciously forgotten. Even in the face of contrary evidence I was still under the power of the word "dumb." *It is not within man to effectively believe against a word planted in his heart.* The "power of Sheol" works through the poor self-image to convince us we "have not" in spite of how much we have. No matter how well we do we still feel like we cannot do well.

A young man, for example, may judge himself to be a failure because he received that word as a child. Two dynamics keep him in constant tension. On the one hand there is the conscious feeling that he should be able to do better—no matter how well he is doing—since he was always told that he could do better if he tried. On the other hand there is the unconscious knowing that he *cannot* do better—no matter how hard he tries—since he was always criticized even when he give it his best shot. That situation creates an internal conflict.

As we have noticed there are many forms of wealth for which a person may strive. We can see this power working in many areas. No matter how much evidence one has that he is successful (whatever that means in any given situation) he knows his T-shirt reads, "Failure." One can always find some standard by which to compare himself so he comes up short. If he's making $4,000 a month there are others making $6,000. If he gets a raise, he compares himself to the one making even more.

One striving for a pay raise may not actually need

more money. Everyone can *use* more, but the desire for more is not necessarily an indication of financial need. *The raise becomes a symbol of acceptance from the boss who has become a father figure to the person in his striving for his natural father's approval.* Even when the raise comes it is never enough to counter the *operative word* that was planted in his heart as a child. The lack of approval is actually coming from within. Having rejected himself he cannot be convinced that anyone else would accept him.

Turning to another form of wealth there are girls who think of themselves as ugly. Often the presence of excessive make-up is an attempt to cover-up (literally) the feeling of being unattractive. This also is a subtle and deceptive power. No matter how beautiful the girl may be, and in spite of compliments and attention, she still feels ugly. She cannot see herself as beautiful because she "knows" what she has covered up. She is driven to find more effective make-up techniques and buy more attractive clothes. She cannot bear the thought of others seeing her as she "really is."

How many are climbing social ladders because they feel unworthy and unacceptable? How many are scholars because they feel dumb? Are there professional football players who are on the field trying to convince themselves they are tough? What about the meticulously clean housekeeper? Is she trying to prove to someone she is a good housekeeper? Or does she really think someone will reject her if they find dust on her furniture? Or under it?

These questions may never have answers. The statistics may never be available. Who can judge whether it is a healthy striving for excellence or a drive for acceptance? As we ask these questions however, the deceptive devices of Sheol are exposed. First we believe a lie and become convinced we are inferior in one way or another. Then for fear of being exposed to others we begin to cover ourselves in some way. When we sense that our cover-up does not change our inner self, we get caught in the undercurrent of looking for more effective cover-up techniques. *We seldom notice the one we are really trying to fool is ourselves.*

Without realizing it we are often trying, and even striving to become something we think are not. While trying to be "something special" we are actually developing into a false-human being.

The undercurrent of "I must" is the power of Sheol whether it be:

> Now I must know,
> I must know,
> Must know,

Or:

> Now I must have,
> I must have,
> Must have,

Or:

> Now I must excel,
> I must excel,
> Must excel….

Seven: A BLOW TO THE HEAD

Three Significant Students

The first year of teaching at Eastern New Mexico University was another significant turning point in my journey. Three distinctively different students contributed to the transition. The battering ram was a young man named Joe. He was big and boisterous with a bellowing baritone voice. He was over six feet tall, almost two hundred pounds of muscles full of anger. His favorite sport was boxing because he could beat people in the face without being arrested. He knew nothing of the meaning of fear.

I think Joe enrolled in my Old Testament Survey class because he wanted to argue with God and I was God's reprehensive. He disrupted every class he attended with his tirade against God. He ranted and raged against God. "If God is good, why is there so much bloodshed in the Bible?" I could almost see the wrestling match between Jacob and the angel (Genesis 32) being reenacted before my eyes. Fortunately for the class he was present only a third of the time. I was able to give the other students a fairly good overview of the Old Testament.

The questions he raised did not shake me and I did not feel threatened by his size or his anger. I knew how to answer the questions from a biblical and theological point of view and I felt confident that my answers were valid. His god-image (what God is like) was inaccurate, and his world-image (how things "ought" to be) was unrealistic.

That was obvious. I even had a measure of insight into the psychological dynamic that drove him to attack God.

Two things about him bothered me. First, I could not get him to be quiet long enough to give him the answers he was demanding. (*The ovum was fighting the seed.*) I told him the answers would come at the appropriate time but he continued to disrupt the class. Second, I knew that even if I could get his attention my answers would not help him with his struggle. His need was too deep to touch with logical explanations. It would take some power beyond academic, logical theology to reach his pain.

I did not know how to respond to his constant barrage of blame and execration against God. Jesus had not defended himself against the reviling of those who crucified him. I knew God was not threatened by this young man's upbraiding. God has no need to defend himself nor did He need me to shield Him from Joe's attacks. *But as long as Joe continued to relate to God through his false image of God the barrier between him and God would remain intact.*

There I was with no way to get his attention and nothing to say but, "God loves you." To Joe's ears that would have sounded like a trite ecclesiastical slogan. Preachers are expected to say that. So *after all those years of seeking and finding answers **my confidence in answers was waning***. During those difficult days I was asking myself whether the answers would ever have any value beyond the classroom. I was equipped to help students fulfill their requirements for a degree, but I had nothing that would touch their real life needs.

This served to focus my attention on what had been happening to me over the years of preparation and training for ministry. In the process of training I had been sidetracked by intellectual pursuits.

The second student was more like a fishing lure than a battering ram. This one came in the person of a student named Astrid. She was enrolled in my class on the Book of Acts and wanted to do her term paper on the phenomenon of speaking in tongues in the early church. Her choice of topics was not unusual. Many students are attracted to the miraculous because of a fascination for the mysterious. What got me was that when she came in for her conference I noticed a sparkle in her eyes that reminded me of the excitement I had known in Japan after Father came to me.

When she handed in her paper to my office at the end of the semester she began to testify of her personal experiences with God. I do not remember any details of what she shared but I will never forget the sense of reality that prevailed as she spoke. For the first time in several years I saw a ray of hope that I might again know the joy of walking daily in God's presence as I had in Japan. I took the bait and began the next leg of my journey.

Having lost confidence in the value of academic information apart from the real presence of God I was ready for something. I needed the same thing the students needed – a deeper personal relationship with the living God. Mere information about God (even if it is true) cannot supply life for students like Joe or for professors like me. With all my striving to find answers, and even finding some, I had come no closer to God. And I had nothing to offer Joe. *Ever-deepening insights into the doctrines of the Bible had failed to yield the quality of life I had known.* I was hungry for what Astrid had.

I began to seek after God with fresh expectation. I had been trained to think my mind was the only faculty available to seek God. I was familiar with Paul's statement, "it is the Spirit himself bearing witness with our spirit that we are children of God," (Romans 8:16). And I knew that "God is Spirit, and those who worship him must worship him in spirit and truth," (John 4:24). But I identified man's spirit with his intellect. *I had developed an image of God as a glorified brain.* I thought an intellectual Bible scholar with strict, disciplined study habits was a spiritual giant. That's dumb.

The second semester of my tenure at Eastern brought the third student into my path. Dick was a graduate student working toward his MA degree in Religion. We quickly became friends during the morning and afternoon coffee breaks. He was the kind of person who liked to talk and who did not seem to notice whether people were listening or not. That bothered me until I started listening. I discovered he was not merely talking; he was actually saying something.

At first the topic of discussion was on some aspect of the graduate class on the Prophets of Israel which I was teaching. My lecture on "the prophetic experience" had included a testimony of the liquid love experience in Japan. My point was that the prophets were not speaking out of their heads but from a real experience of the presence of the real God. In our dialogue I sensed he understood what I was talking about better than the other students, perhaps better than me.

As our relationship developed other subjects often came up in our conversation. He had a unique ability to address questions without knowing I was wrestling with those very questions privately. At first I attributed that to the fact that he just liked to talk and should be expected to ramble into a topic I was studying sooner or later. But it happened so often that I began to suspect it was more than mere coincidence.

One day I was in my office studying Hebrews 4:12 where it speaks of the living and active word of God dividing the soul and spirit. My training had led me to believe that the soul and spirit were essentially the same thing. I had also identified the phrase "word of God" with the written text of the Bible. The image of man's mind actively engaging the text did not seem to fit this text in Hebrews. The greater difficulty for me was the *division* of soul and spirit. How could that which is the "same thing" be divided? I also wondered what the function of the written text in that process might be.

As I was turning this problem over in my mind there was a knock at the door. It was Dick. He came in, seated himself and began to explain the difference between soul and spirit. I listened with my feet propped up on the desk as he proceeded to answer all my questions one by one. During this one-sided conversation I never once gave any indication that he was touching a topic I was seriously grappling with just before he came in. He just kept rambling (very systematically) until all my questions were answered.

I had been approaching the issue of seeking after God with the wrong faculty. The mind of man is a function of the soul and is distinctly different from the spirit of man. When Peter confessed that Jesus was the Christ, Jesus said, "Flesh and blood has not revealed this to you, but my Father who is in heaven," (Matthew 16:17). In other words, Peter did not figure that out by logical analysis. It came into his human spirit from the Father.

Many bright and doctrinally informed Pharisees failed to receive that revelation because they approached Jesus through human logic. The "spirit of your mind" (Ephesians 4:23) receives understanding through an act of God. The living and active word does its work in the human spirit, not the soul. "He who belongs to the Lord is one spirit with him" (I Corinthians 6:17). Just as man and woman become one so we become one with the Lord. That means we have access to Him through our human spirit as we open ourselves to His work within our spirit.

As Dick was drawing his comments to a close my curiosity was aroused as never before. How was it possible for him to consistently answer questions, week after week, without knowing I was asking those questions privately? So I asked what had motivated him to come by the office and speak of this topic at this time. He said, "The Holy Spirit prompted me to leave what I was doing and come share these thoughts with you."

I knew him to be an excellent student. He was not a "flakey" person so I was not expecting an answer involving the Holy Spirit. I do not know if he noticed it or not but I was in total shock when he left. I could not understand how a young man of his ability and perceptivity could make such a non-rational statement.

Being intellectually stimulated by the whole question of the Holy Spirit's involvement in man's daily life I picked up some paperback testimonials from the bookstore and began to read. Many interesting and exciting experiences were shared in those books but, since I had no doctrinal cubbyhole to place them in, I was

95

discounting most of what I read. I would never have called my approach unbelief. But it turned out that *I was an **unbelieving believer***.

The church of my youth had never spoken of the Holy Spirit as a viable influence in a person's life today. It was like He inspired the Bible and went back to heaven to see how we would handle it. If anything about the Holy Spirit influencing our daily decisions was ever taught in my college days I had not had ears to hear it. This was a completely new idea to me and it was stretching my theological wineskin to the breaking point.

Dethroning the Intellect

These three, Joe, Astrid and Dick, were instrumental in drawing my attention to this area of need in my life. Slowly I began to see that man must seek after God with his spirit, not with his mind, because God is Spirit. I was relieved to recognize that I would not have to understand God before he could move in my life again. But I was helpless to break free from the intellectual whirlpool that held me hostage in its vortex. I did not yet know how to connect with my spirit and allow the Holy Spirit to lead. The question, "How does one yield to the Spirit?" was now my quest.

The more I read the more I desired the reality of it all. But at the same time my well trained rational mind was supplying more convincing reasons why it could not possibly be true. I was learning by experience that "the desires of the flesh are against the desires of the Spirit, and the desires of the Spirit are against the flesh," (Galatians 5:17). Every effort of the flesh (my natural

96

abilities apart from God) took me farther away from the reality I so desperately wanted. The ovum in me was also resisting the seed. Japan and the experience of love were still "*once upon a time, in a land far away.*"

I had not noticed that the experience in Japan did not come as a result of any effort on my part. In this case also, all my efforts were of no avail. *The turning in Japan was an event that happened to me* apart from any human effort or understanding. Like Saul of Tarsus I was actually resisting it at the time. Now in New Mexico I was trying my best to maintain my balance in the tornado that was sucking me up. I never suspected that Father was the one drawing me back to Himself.

I was reading a book late at night when it happened. It was the testimony of Pat Boone, *A New Song.* My mind was explaining away each successive story as it came page after page. My reservations were never consciously identified as unbelief any more than Saul would have recognized his zeal was directed against the very God he thought he was serving. I felt it was my responsibility before God to explain away these stories to protect the young students from being carried away into the false doctrines of this new sect of the Holy Spirit.

While I was reading and explaining everything away suddenly, without warning, the Lord appeared in the room. It was not the sweet presence of "liquid love" as it had been in Japan, though it was a very gentle Presence. *This time He appeared as LORD in the full meaning of the term.* The Presence evoked a sense of holy awe. It was a kind of fear I had known as a child. The presence was not frightening; it was kingly, overpowering, awe-full. I "saw" Him out of the corner of my mind's eye. I think I could have counted the locks of His hair if I had looked squarely at him. But I dared not look.

Not knowing what to do I asked, "Is that you, Lord?" I do not know why I asked. There was no doubt in my mind it was He. The moment I asked He spoke to me deep in my spirit. It was not a speaking to my conscious mind so I did not know what He said. I only knew He had spoken. I began to cry and sob. The words "I'm sorry, I'm sorry," kept coming out of my mouth from deep within. I did not know what I was apologizing for but I knew it had something to do with what He said to me deep within. The word-seed had penetrated the ovum of my spirit.

The weeping continued for about half an hour. Afterward I felt very clean and there was a new freshness inside. Whatever it was that happened, it was real and effective on a very deep level. What He said had come to the ovum my spirit as a "living and active word," a word that accomplished its intended work within my spirit even without my conscious awareness of what He had spoken. The process of the dividing of my soul from my spirit began when He spoke that living word to my spirit.

There was a new zest for life just as there had been when He came with His loving acceptance while I was in the Air Force. Things began to change so rapidly that I have trouble piecing together a chronological sequence of how it all came about. I did not understand what had happened or what it was all supposed to mean, but I knew He had not come to give understanding; He had come to bring me out of death (separation) into life in the Spirit. He was dividing my soul from my spirit.

There is one thing I did understand. He who had come to me as Love, who accepted me in my backsliding, had now shown Himself as the one having all authority in heaven and on earth. In Japan He had revealed His *unconditional love*. In New Mexico He revealed His *unconditional lordship. It was the **lordship of His love***. It was not raw authority. It was the loving concern of the one who died and was raised for my justification.

The soul is designed to be a servant of the spirit. But our culture trains the soul from early childhood and either waits till the child is in puberty to speak to his spirit or never speaks to his spirit at all. The result is that our mind is "made up" and our will is stubborn by the time anyone addresses our spirit. We neglect the human spirit in our determination to have successful children who know how to make decisions and follow through – apart from God.

During the next few months I read everything I could get my hands on dealing with the Holy Spirit as a present and active reality in the lives of Christians (*My reading problem had been healed*). My eyes had somehow been opened to see things in a new light.

The Greek word translated "repentance" actually means "to see things differently, to experience a change in how you think." I had repented of my unbelief that night when He appeared as Lord. I began to think differently. Now I understood that it was the Holy Spirit who had made the presence of the Father so real in Japan. The problem was that I had not learned to relate the experience in Japan to my life as a whole.

The experience of liquid love was something that happened "once upon a time." I saw no need to integrate that experience into my theology except as an illustration of how the biblical prophets received from God. In the process of receiving an education I had come to think of it as subject matter for academic investigation rather than something to provide a dynamic for daily living. It had come to be little more than an illustration to add a personal touch to my teaching.

That was all beginning to change now and I was excited again. The first obvious change was in the area of Bible reading. After visiting with Dick until about nine p.m. one evening I decided to read a while as I waited for him to return. I knew he would return because he left his wife who was visiting with my wife in another room. I opened the Bible to the book of Romans and began to read. The book came alive. It was as though I had never read it before in my whole life. I had taken Romans in undergraduate school and had translated the entire book from the Greek as a graduate student. I had even taught through the book on the college level.

This time it was different. My spirit was eating the Bread of Life as I read. Life was coming to me from every page. After completing Romans, I moved on to the Corinthian letters then to Galatians and Ephesians. Every word was alive and breathing. I continued to read until I had finished all of Paul's letters. At 2:00 a.m. I finally put the Bible down as Dick walked in to pick up his wife. Something very real was happening as I read. Later I came to realize that the division of soul and spirit had prepared me to receive the living and active word of God.

The Problem Exposed

Without realizing it I had picked up a spirit of intellectualism in the process of striving for an education. In using knowledge as a cover-up for a poor self-image I had exalted logic to the throne of my life. My mind had begun to usurp the authority and function of the Holy Spirit as though my natural mind could lead me in the ways of God and into the truth that comes only by the Father's act of revealing. I had made a covenant with intellectualism without knowing it.

My intellect was a "covenant partner" and protected me from exposure as a Dumb-Dumb *in exchange for the right to censure everything that passed through my psyche*. This "friend" would not allow anything to come from my inner spirit into consciousness without some re-definition or logical qualification. It was this intellectual spirit that had been explaining away everything I read in the testimonials.

The spirit in me that had been begotten of the "living and abiding word of God" (I Peter 1:23) was suffering from malnutrition. My natural mind would not allow any "word-milk" (I Peter 2:2) to pass through the circuits of the logical censuring process. That is why all my attempts to break through to God had ended in failure. *But now God had broken through to me.* He triumphed over my intellectualism and established Himself as Lord in my heart. The new (original) me was emerging.

While reading Paul's letters and receiving life through his words *God was uncovering Himself* to me by His Spirit. All my previous attempts to discover (uncover) God were in vain – fruitless. Now I understand what Paul meant when he said the "letter kills, but the Spirit gives life" (II Corinthians 3:6). That night, with unveiled face, I beheld the "glory of the Lord" while reading Scripture (II Corinthians 3:18). He removed the veil for me and made Himself known.

Over a period of time I began to have more confidence in the unsolicited insights that came during my private Bible study. The sharing of these insights brought life to the students. I knew there was reality in what I was seeing. It was not long before I even had the opportunity to pray for Joe (who had given me such a hard time in Old Testament Survey). Seeing him on his knees in my living room asking Jesus to be Lord of his life was a touching sight indeed.

As the process of dethroning the intellect continued various thoughts and insights continued to gurgle up from deep within me. These insights bubbled up from the same place the sobbing and crying had come from when He revealed His lordship to me. As I became more sensitive to those musings of my spirit I could even hear the words He spoke to me that night when He revealed His lordship. The words spoken several months earlier were still echoing in my spirit. He had said, "Fount, you have not been believing me, have you?"

There was no condemnation in His voice, only loving concern for me. It is no wonder I was sobbing and saying "I'm sorry, I'm sorry." My spirit was grieving because my unbelief had grieved Father's Spirit. The power of the living and active word of God had done a deep work in my spirit and I saw things differently i.e., I repented. The wall between my soul and my spirit crumbled so the sense of the presence of the Lord could become conscious.

Since that time there has never been any doubt in my mind that there is a difference between the soul and spirit of man. After years of trying to find God with my mind my spirit heard the voice of the Lord and responded in repentance while my conscious mind was confused. I knew I was not having a breakdown because I was at peace within myself. I was fully aware of my conscious thoughts while something deep was happening that caused the deep recesses of my spirit to erupt.

His words had entered effectively into my spirit but had no admittance into my conscious mind until the intellectual spirit was no longer erected as a barrier. The fact that those words were still almost audibly present in my spirit was to me a sign of the reality of the distinction between the soul and spirit. I came to realize that one can be born of the Spirit without walking by the Spirit. A major motivation in my academic training was an attempt to gratify the desire of my flesh – to have a place of honor in this world as an academic, "smart" person.

It is true that the two words, soul (*psyche*) and spirit (*pneuma*) both refer to the inner man as distinct from the outward man. When the context calls for a clear distinction, however, the word flesh (*sarx*) refers to man's soulish nature in its opposition to the Spirit of God. In this context flesh does not refer to the meaty portion of the physical body. The desires of the flesh are not limited to the impulses and cravings of the physical body. The works of the flesh (*sarx*) include strife, enmity, jealousy, anger, selfishness etc. (Galatians 5:20). *My desire to cover up the Dumb-Dumb self-image and to look like a spiritual giant was a desire of the flesh.*

This concept clarifies Paul's question in Galatians 3:3, "Are you so foolish? Having begun with the Spirit, are you now being perfected with the flesh?" My walk with the Lord had been initiated by the Spirit in Japan but I had been trying to bring myself to maturity by my own natural abilities. I was trying to proclaim the testimony of

God in lofty words of wisdom. No wonder there was no "demonstration of the Spirit and of power," (I Corinthians 2:1-5). Having placed my faith in human wisdom no power of life was available through my teaching.

Adam's death (separation) came when he fell out of relationship with God. Sin separated him from the source of true life. We received the human nature—the nature created in the image of God—when we were born physically. We fall out of relationship with God when we begin to yield to our earthly appetites and become resistant to the things of the Spirit. But all this activity can only produce death in the sense of being out of touch with the source of true life. There can be no fruit for God from the seed of Adam (see fig. #4).

Jesus Christ, "being raised from the dead will never die again; death no longer has dominion over him. For the death he died he died to sin, once for all but the life he lives he lives to God" (Romans 6:9-10). Adam's death was death to the influence of God. He lived under the influence of the lie that he must become like God by his own power. During his life Jesus was dead to this lie and His life was lived under the influence of God. Just as we participate in Adam's death when we receive the lie, so we participate in Christ's life when we receive the truth and experience spiritual birth. The lifeline to God was reconnected by the work of Jesus Christ.

It is foolish to try to establish a relationship with God through the natural mind. That is what Eve tried to do. When she believed the Serpent's lie, she came to a logical conclusion: "To be like God one must disregard the instructions of God." Her response to that lie created a barrier between her spirit and the Spirit of God.

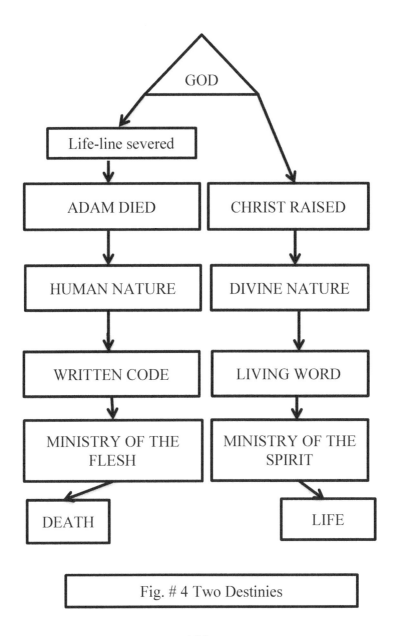

Fig. # 4 Two Destinies

105

We can read the Bible and find accurate doctrines and clear definitions of the life we *ought* to live, but we receive no power to do what we know is right. Even if one could muster up enough self-discipline to produce good outward behavior he will only have cleansed the outside of the cup. The inside could still be full of greed and self-indulgence (Matthew 23:25). He would be a good Pharisee. That is all.

When a man turns to the Lord the veil of the flesh is removed and he is able to receive the living and active word of God. That word transforms him from one degree of glory to another. As the soulish man is dethroned and the Spirit of God takes His rightful place in our lives, the new man in Christ emerges. As we walk by the Spirit we can say with Paul, "It is no longer I who live, but Christ who lives in me," (Galatians 2:20). This life becomes a manifestation of the sons of God (Romans 8:19).

When the intellect was dethroned in my life, I did not lose my ability to analyze and exercise logic. It is just that that aspect of my person was no longer the final authority for me. *My intellect was no longer my god.*

In the next three chapters we'll turn our attention to the process of receiving the living and active word. Our question will be, "How does a person receive this living word in such a way that he or she begins to manifest the life of God in the earth?" From the above story it should be obvious that human effort can never break through. (Actually He is not trying to keep us out anyway.) But there is a position we can take that will allow Him to break through our cognitive bias. He broke through mine.

Eight: THE IMPLANTED WORD

Review

We have noticed that seed reproduces after its own kind. The nature of the offspring is determined by the seed of its generation. We inherited our human nature with the image of God from Adam (primal man) through the mediation of our parents. We have also noticed that our self-image develops through receiving a formative word from important others during childhood. That word (in my case Dumb-Dumb) effects the development of behavior patterns and attitudes.

We divided behavior patterns into two categories: 1) Cover-up and 2) Exposure. In the first case one is trying to hide what he considers to be his true nature (his T-shirt) lest he be rejected. In the second case he is exposing himself (unconsciously perhaps) in an attempt to find someone who will love him for who he really is. He is looking for a home where he can belong, where he is loved. It seems universal among us that we feel like we are homeless. We spend our lives looking for a home, for a place of belonging without having to change or perform.

Next we discovered that when one is begotten of the living and abiding word of God he receives a seed from above which awakens his original (new) nature with the capacity to reflect the image of God (Romans 8:29). In this chapter we are on our way to noticing a third category of behavior that moves us toward our new (yet original) destiny. This changes everything. We have a "*renewed who*." It may take a lifetime to discover this new creature

107

who is "created after the likeness of God in true righteousness and holiness" (Ephesians 4:24). But it is there in us even if we do not recognize it.

The story line of every pilgrim's life revolves around attempts to discover his or her true identity and relationship to the Source of life, to nature and to other people. We began this book with the question, "Who am I really?" In this chapter we turn our attention to the process of receiving the self-image that comes with the seed of the Word of God. Within this seed is the potential of becoming "partakers of the divine nature" (II Peter 1:4). We do not realize what that means until we join other travelers on the same journey. *We learn who we are as we walk on the path together with fellow pilgrims.* There are always others. No one is alone.

Moving Forward

My journey began in all seriousness when I was homesick in Japan. The home I was missing, the home I was looking for, was the place Jesus prepared for us in His Father's bosom. After He came to me as liquid love I knew I was a new man but had no idea what that meant. The battle between my old (false) nature and my new (true) nature began as I tried to discover reality through a formal education. There was an inner restlessness under the surface of all my striving for knowledge. As it turns out the restlessness was an unconscious awareness that I was not yet embracing my true identity.

The next major transition for me was the experience of His lordship in New Mexico. The B.A. never satisfied me. The M.A. failed to give me rest. The Ph.D. left me with a holy dissatisfaction that drove me (or drew me) toward the original and radical intimacy with God that first found expression in Japan as liquid love. The experience in New Mexico created a deep longing for home but this time I was longing for the full realization of the home I found when He filled the barrack room with His love. The bosom of Father is my original home even before I entered my earthly father's house. I really belong here. *Father created **in me** a longing for what he had prepared **for me** while I was in my mother's womb.*

This is not an easy journey because our enemy is into identity theft. The enemy wants to keep us confused lest we become a threat to the "kingdom of darkness" as sons and daughters of light. But every true pilgrim will discover that our Father uses the enemy's resistance to help us develop into the persons we already are in Christ. As in weightlifting, resistance is necessary for growth and development. In one sense we are not really becoming something new. We are emerging from the seed which contained the whole from the very beginning. All the "spiritual organs, bones and muscles" were already there in the original seed.

Our feeling of homelessness creates a restlessness that urges us forward through the road blocks of life. The problem is that we tend to think the enemy is the devil, society, the government or "those people who are wrong." *On the journey we discover that **we are our own worst enemy**.* We hinder ourselves by trying to cover up a false image of ourselves. In this way we simply develop another false image. We strive to be something we were not created to be and in so doing we block the growth of the implanted word from Father God.

In the process of dethroning the intellect I began to realize that Father had given me a "coat of many colors" like Jacob gave to Joseph (Genesis 37:3). I actually believe He gives everyone an amazing coat. One of the "colors" of my coat is analytical abilities and another is a sense of humor. I had been using my analytical abilities to cover the fact that I felt dumb and my humor to maneuver my way through life without help from above. By continuing to listen to the internalized voice of my dad I was failing to properly display the coat. I was wearing my self-constructed metal armor instead.

I also noticed that one major problem in our society is a particular notion of success. The word success often implies a place where we will have finally arrived. When we arrive at the place we *thought* would be success we are only content for a time. Then we begin to strive for the next higher place. It might be more and more degrees, as it was with me, or it might be higher and higher levels on the corporate ladder. *When we get to the top we often discover we have put the ladder against the wrong building.*

Then I noticed that I had been trying to engineer my own transformation by my intellect and human wisdom rather than allowing myself to be transformed by the power of the Spirit of God (Romans 12:2). I was becoming a "Bible-thumper" trying to tell everyone else how to change while my Father was trying to change me. The ego that was trying to transform itself is the ego that needed transformation. *Gravity keeps us from lifting ourselves by our own bootstraps.*

Like Joseph I now choose to honor my Father by wearing the coat he gave me even though it may trouble some people. I had not been wearing that coat partly because I did not even know it was there. But more significant was my fear that people would think I was being arrogant. During the process of "taking off" the armor I would not even allow people to call me Dr. Shults. I preferred to be called Brother Fount. I do not need the title to feel good about myself, but I will *no longer dishonor my Father by putting the coat in the closet* to avoid the "Sheol" of separation. As it turns out I really am "smart" just like my teachers had told my mom.

As the old self-image developed through receiving a formative word from my earthly father so my new self-image continues to develop as I receive words of insight from Father God, words which are able to bring my soul to health and wholeness (James 1:21). Let me explain.

The Word was in the beginning with God and became flesh in the person of Jesus Christ (John 1:1, 14). Within His "spiritual loins" is the word-seed which is now available to all mankind through the resurrection. When we receive that word-seed into our spirit (like an ovum) through reading or hearing the word, it begins to grow and develop within us. Just as a seed begins its growth underground, so the development of our "renewed who" happens unconsciously at first. As toddlers in the natural we gradually became aware of ourselves and the world we live in. In the same way we slowly become aware of ourselves as new creatures in Christ.

As the original, true nature becomes aware of itself in its spiritual environment it can begin to receive word-seeds from the Father in heaven. The new words from our new (original) Father become the formative element in our next level of growth and development as a child

111

begotten of God (John 1:13). Peter was speaking of this when he wrote, "like new born babes, long for the pure word-milk, that by it you may grow up to salvation," (I Peter 2:2).

Word-Milk and Expression-Behavior

The phrase "word-milk" in some versions is "spiritual milk." A comparison will show the significance of this phrase. A baby produced by canine-seed we call a puppy. That puppy is hungry for dog-milk. Dog-milk causes the puppy to grow into a mature dog. A baby produced by feline seed we call a kitten. The kitten is hungry for cat-milk so it can grow into a mature cat. Both the kitten and the puppy are hungry for milk produced by the one that produced them.

A baby produced by word-seed we can call a baby word. That baby word is hungry for word-milk. When we are begotten of the seed of the living and active word of God we are born hungry for the milk produced by the one who produced us. Word-milk causes the baby word to grow into a mature word. We can all say, *"When I grow up I'll be a full grown expression (word) of what Father God has to say to this generation through my life."* I will become more and more a manifestation of His divine life as I grow and mature. (More on this in a later chapter.)

Many problems in life are a result of trying to *live up to* a destiny received from words given by our parents. Some words imply we are something *other than what we really are by nature* – like trying to become a lawyer when you are really an artist. Trying to live up to the expectations of others is very frustrating. It keeps us from

112

developing our true nature. Other problems come from trying to **live down** *words that imply we are less than we are by nature* (like Dumb-Dumb). In either case the struggle comes from the inconsistency between what we receive from the divine word-seed and what we receive from human words. The image of God in us can only grow as we receive with meekness the word-milk.

On the right side of figure #3 in a chapter 3 (p. 67) there is no inconsistency between the nature we receive from the word-seed and the image we receive from the words spoken by our Father. On the right side of that chart the Word (which is God himself) is both the seed and the nourishment for the new man in Christ. The word our heavenly Father speaks to us is consistent with the Word of our regeneration. Since this word generates and nurtures the divine nature within us there is nothing in our new (original) image to cause shame.

Many times I would ask students, "What would others see if they saw the deepest thing in you?" When their insecurities rose up I would say, "*There is no need to hide because the deepest thing in you is the divine nature.*" When we express ourselves as we really are in Christ what others see is Christ in us, the hope of glory (Colossians 1:27). We do not need to "*expose*" ourselves to find someone who loves us unconditionally. We can now "*express*" our true selves because we ARE loved unconditionally, and we know it. When this new man behaves according to his nature, his life is a manifestation of the God who IS Love.

This "expression" is our third category of behavior. Our behavior becomes an expression of the divine nature.

The Problem

The problem is that the old and the new live in the same body. The fleshly tendency and the spiritual nature are "in conflict with each other to keep you from doing the things you want to do" (Galatians 5:17). In other words, our false image is against our true nature. It is possible for both blessings and curses to come from the same mouth because there are two springs inside, one pouring forth fresh water and the other brackish (James 3:10-11). It ought not to be so, but it is a fact of life. There is a war, an internal conflict between flesh and spirit within us to determine *which source will supply our mouth with words and our body with actions*. We choose.

Problems develop when we choose to manifest "stuff" (like more money, more impressive knowledge or higher levels of influence) to cover our erroneous image of who we are. We try to use our personality and abilities to gain "stuff" to hide how we really feel about ourselves deep inside. The "new man" has been there since we received the word-seed waiting for us to reject our fear of rejection and our desire for supremacy so that our true nature might emerge. We begin to live the abundant life of dominion over everything negative when we do this.

The objective of the new man in Christ is to "put off" the old self with its corrupt behavior patterns and to "put on the new self, created after the likeness of God in true righteousness and holiness," (Ephesians 4:22-24). The process of growing spiritually involves *taking off* the armors, the overcoats, the three-piece suits and even the T-shirts of our concocted self-image. That is the negative. The positive aspect of the process is *putting on* (slipping

114

into) the reality of who we are in Christ Jesus.

Behavior patterns come from the word-based images we adopt as our self-concept. If the words we receive are consistent with the divine nature, our behavior will reflect the glory of Christ. But if the words we receive are inconsistent with or contradictory to the divine nature our behavior will reflect the false nature with its passions and desires. Many passions, like quoting Bible verses or doing good deeds, look very good on the surface. But as we have said, flesh is flesh and can produce only flesh.

The problem clearly stated is that *the false self is already well established in its images and habitual behavior before the true nature comes to consciousness.* As we become aware of our true nature the false self often tries to produce the "true righteousness and holiness" by fleshly strength and wisdom without really knowing what true righteousness is. That is the essence of religious legalism. Having begun in the Spirit we try to mature through the activity of the flesh (Galatians 3:3). Righteous deeds produced by the false self are filthy rags (Isaiah 64:6). "Filthy rags" here is probably a reference to the rags of the menstrual cycle where the unfertilized egg is passed. No real life will result from that activity.

Only the Divine nature in us can produce true righteousness. That which is flesh is flesh and can at best only produce a religious pretense. Man as man can only produce images of God from the vain imaginations of his heart. Any holiness produced by the flesh is a holiness that reflects a god which is a no god (cf. Jeremiah16:20). The flesh cannot create a god which is real; neither can it produce a godliness that is true holiness. In my opinion atheism is a negative response to the attempts of many to

115

give intellectual, logical proofs of God or to produce the divine-nature without help from the true God.

The Promise

On the other hand, Father God has given us the right and the ability to become children of God (John 1:13). The divine nature in those who receive the word-seed is predestined to be conformed to the image of the first-born Son (Romans 8:29). Like the oak in the acorn we have the potential of sharing and reflecting His glory (Romans 8:28). This is not the vain expectation of the human ego; it is a promise of Father to those who follow the Spirit's leading (Romans 8:14). *Being a son or daughter of God becomes both an inner reality and an outward way of living life as we follow the Spirit*. In this way we begin to manifest our true sonship.

Father God offers a positive work (putting on the new) and a negative work (putting off the old) in our behavior. He and He alone can accomplish both sides of this work. We can do neither apart from Him.

When it is "no longer I who live, but Christ who lives in me" (Galatians 2:20), the Christ in me can and will live a life of true righteousness and holiness. He is the only one who can live that life. When it is He who lives His life in me it is not pretense. It is the presence of the Father abiding in the new man (John 14:20-24). ***The God who demands holiness*** in our conduct (I Peter 1:15) also ***provides the holiness He requires***. He develops holiness in us as we allow the Christ in us to unfold and express Himself. He is our only hope of glory (Colossians 1:27). This is Father's positive work in us.

To enter the kingdom of God *we must abdicate the throne of our own personal kingdom*. The problem of the true and the false both seeking expression through the same body is insurmountable apart from a continuing work of God. This is where his negative work comes in. It is only by the Spirit that we are able to put to death the deeds of the body (Romans 8:13). The Spirit overcomes every obstacle in those who are willing to lay down their self-life and follow the leading of the Spirit. As the old dies the new begins to live. *Both the dying and the living are a work of the One who placed the divine nature in us.*

It is encouraging to know that, "though our false self is wasting away, our true self is being renewed every day" (II Corinthians 4:16). Even though the old self had a head start it is fighting a losing battle in those who are willing to die to themselves and come alive to God. Jesus lived his life unto God as one who had died to sin (Romans 6:10). As we allow Him to live His life in us we are dead to sin and alive to God. Although our new man *can* allow sin to reign in his mortal bodies (Romans 6:12), he is *no longer bound* to miss the mark of true holiness.

Our new life is hidden with Christ in God (Colossians 3:3). In the beginning this new life is hidden even from us. As we mature in Christ we become more and more aware of the life that is already working in us apart from our awareness. *We do not create the new life; we simply recognize it as it unfolds within us.* It unfolds as we grow in our willingness and ability to see what Father is doing in us and join Him in His agenda.

The pilgrim's journey is a passing over one threshold after another and entering new levels of maturity through experiencing God's presence and activity in and through

117

our daily lives. The divine nature in us becomes our new (yet original) identity. The fullness of God dwells in us and expresses itself through us to the degree that we submit to the still, small voice of the Spirit within us.

The Nature of the Journey

The journey is like a spiral staircase. We do not move forward in a straight line. As we move toward our destiny of being conformed to the image of Christ we come to the East side of the staircase. We return to the East side again later as we continue but this time we are on a higher level. The growth usually happens without our conscious awareness. It is like we wake up one day and realize we have arrived at a higher and deeper life in the Spirit.

"See what manner of love the Father has given to us, that we should be called children of God; and so we are," John wrote (I John 3:1). Then he continued, "What we will be has not yet appeared; but we know that when he appears we will be like him, because we will see him as he is" (I John 3:2). *What we are **able to see** determines what we are **able to be**.* In other words, I do not know exactly what I will look like when I "grow up" spiritually because I have not yet seen Him in the fullness of who He is. I have not yet fully grasped the reality of who He is; therefore, I do not yet know what it means to be like Him.

We come to see Him more clearly as we allow His Spirit to express itself in our lived-life. Merely seeing Him in a new way creates a new level of likeness in us. As we have more experiences of His divine life manifesting itself in us, we see His nature expressed in our words and actions more often, more clearly, and more

118

effectively. We begin to manifest the life of Christ.

Though Scripture clearly indicates that He will someday appear in a full revelation and manifestation of who He is, we can and do have many experiences of His appearing to us in new ways as we move forward on our personal journey. For example, He appeared to me as liquid love in Japan and later as Lord in New Mexico. Each appearance was a deeper revelation of His nature. When I saw Him in this new way something in me came to another level of maturity. I did not realize it at that time, but there was much more to come.

We dis-cover ourselves in Him as He dis-covers Himself in us. We find out **who we are** as He shows us **who He is**. This seeing (dis-covering) is not a result of academic pursuit. We may be pursuing a deeper understanding of life when He uncovers Himself to us, but apart from His work of opening our blind eyes we will never see what needs to be seen no matter how diligently we study. When Paul said "God works together in all things for the good of those who love Him" (Romans 8:28), he indicated that Father uses even hard situations in our life to bring us to a deeper revelation of Himself.

The story of the prodigal son is a picture of the pilgrim's journey. Before he began his journey back to his father's house the prodigal "came to himself" (Luke 15:17). The phrase "came to himself" implies that he was not being himself or that he was "beside himself." What brought him to his senses was the sudden realization that the father he had rejected was a good father. He did not *become* a son at that point; he suddenly realized he *was* the son of a good father who took very good care of his servants. With that revelation he began his journey back to his father's house.

But his journey into the awareness of his father's goodness was not yet complete. He intended to request a position among his father's servants because he knew his father took care of his servants. In other words, he knew he was the son of a *good father*, but he did not yet grasp the significance of *his sonship*. He thought he would have to work his way into his father's favor by laboring on the farm. He was on his way to becoming like his elder brother who worked in the father's field as a servant to earn his father's favor. Elder brother was laboring to earn the right to have a party in the house that belonged to him.

The goodness of the father—who represents our Father God—is demonstrated when he did not require his wayward son to do penance before allowing him to come into the house. His father gave him shoes for his feet (so he could walk as a son), a ring for his finger (the authority of a son), and a robe (of righteousness) so he could enter the house and enjoy the celebration of his return. These are all gifts our Father gives apart from any work done by the His sons and daughters. That is how good our Father is. (For a more complete discussion of the prodigal son see my book, *Invitation to Intimacy.*)

Our Father's intention is to bring believers to conformity to the image of his first-born Son. Jesus came to bring "many sons to glory," (Hebrews 2:10). Father's desire is to bring all His sons to a level of maturity where they reflect the Father's glory in both their character and in their conduct. The basic desire of true fatherhood is to have a house full of sons and daughters who bear his image and likeness in their attitude, conduct and relationships. Father God wants sons and daughters who manifest His divine life here in this world.

It is also true that every son or daughter has the capacity to grow into the likeness of the father of the family (in this case the divine Parent). Our destiny is to be conformed to the image of the "God-Man" Jesus Christ. When we focus on "heaven someday" we risk missing the real goal of our journey. That goal is to allow the divine nature to develop into a full expression of sonship in us. "Thy will be done in earth as in heaven," means allowing ourselves to be a channel for heaven's reality to become manifest in our lived-life on the earth.

He created humanity in His image. He is still in the process of bringing that image into a more evident expression through the lives of those who are willing to receive the word-seed, drink the word-milk and allow Him to live His life through them. Too many of us choose the tree of the knowledge of good and evil over the tree of life. Knowledge here means personal experience. Obviously we err when we intentionally choose to experience and promote destructive behavior. But even the knowledge of good is deficient if that goodness does not come from the tree of life, from Father's life in us.

Biblically speaking there is more involved in salvation than a promise of heaven after we die. Eternal life is more than continued existence over an infinitely long period of time. Eternity is a quality of life. It will continue forever but without the quality it is not an exciting prospect. Consider this: "would you like to live forever in the condition you are in right now?" With this question it becomes clear that eternal life has to be a quality of life rather than a mere continuation.

Even if you are in a good place physically and

emotionally, or even spiritually, there is a higher quality of life available. *Any teaching that offers "heaven someday" with no power to live a life of godliness here and now is only a partial gospel.* The full gospel includes what Ruth Paxon called life on the highest plain. That life is available here and now as well as there and then.

Jesus said, "Whoever believes in the Son has eternal life" (John 3:36). He offers a present reality; He offers eternal life *here and now* not merely *someday up there*. The eternal life Jesus offers is His own abundant life. It is the life of Christ, the divine nature in us manifested here and now. It will continue eternally but its present reality is in this life. God's goal is to bring heaven to earth. Bob Mumford once commented, "Getting people to heaven is easy: Get them saved and shoot them. But getting heaven into people requires their cooperation."

That is why Jesus taught us to pray "Your kingdom come, your will be done on earth as it is in heaven." The will of God being done on earth IS heaven coming to earth in and through the lives of His sons and daughters who allow the divine life to manifest through them.

We began by exposing the **problem** of the false man and the true man living in the same body. Then we recognized the **promise** of the Father to bring us to a level of maturity where we reflect His glory in our character and conduct. In the next chapter we will discover the Father's **program**, His method of working this character into us and bringing forth through us the conduct that becomes true righteousness and holiness.

Nine: THE SALVATION OF THE SOUL

The popular concept of salvation is that we receive something like a ticket to heaven when we say the "sinner's prayer." It is as though we think, "When the heaven bus comes, I will be allowed to board and go to heaven." Thinking of heaven and salvation in this way is blocking many from an abundant life here and now. Our concept of salvation obviously needs serious adjustment, especially when we read James 1:18-22 with ears to hear and eyes to see what the text is really saying. James identified his readers as those who by the will of God have been brought forth [born] by the word of truth." Then he directs those born-of-the-word believers to receive with meekness the implanted word *"which is able to save your souls."*

James is saying that these born again persons are still in need of something to save their souls. So being born of the word of truth is not strictly equal to what James calls the salvation of the soul. The experience of being justified (born again) is the beginning but in this chapter we will notice that salvation is a continuing process of growing and maturing for those who are born into Father's family.

A closer look at Peter's writings gives the same impression. Having stated that we have been born again he allows that we may be "grieved by various trials" so that our faith may be tested as by fire. The goal of the testing is that, "as the result of your faith you may obtain the salvation of your souls," (I Peter 1:3-9). Those who are born anew apparently have not yet obtained the salvation of their souls. *If salvation is by grace, it is*

123

something given; we don't need to obtain it. We all face trials in life but in the midst of the trials we can look forward to something called the salvation of our souls on the other side of the suffering that tests our faith.

If that is true, and it is, then salvation is something that happens to us here in this world as we mature in our ability to manifest the divine nature in our conduct and relationships. We need a more complete understanding of these two key words soul and salvation.

Salvation

The root idea of the word translated salvation is found in the context of physical healing. When Jairus came to Jesus his daughter was at the point of death. He asked Jesus to come lay his hands on her that she might be made well and live (Mark 5:23). The word translated "made well" here is *sozo*. It is the same word James and Peter used above for salvation. The same word appears later in the healing of the woman with the issue of blood. When she touched the hem of His garment she was made well (*sozo*) or saved (Mark 5:34).

One is "saved" when rescued or delivered from a difficult or dangerous situation and brought into safety. The word pictures a state of wellbeing in which the one delivered is not only free from the danger but also safe from any continuing harm or lingering after-effects. There is both an immediate and an ongoing aspect of being saved. The daughter of Jairus was not only rescued from the negative work of death, she was also brought into a state of positive health and wholeness to continue her life. The woman was delivered from the issue of blood and given health and wellbeing so she could live fully.

With this understanding of salvation as healing, the statements of James and Peter begin to make more sense. As the newborn babe begins to receive the implanted word (James. 1:21), or the milk of the word (I Peter. 2:2), the soul experiences a deliverance from bondage and comes into an ever improving condition of health and wholeness. *As the physical body begins to function properly after a healing, so the soul can begin to function properly under the leadership of the Spirit when it is healed (saved).* We experience the ongoing effects of the salvation of our souls as the implanted word brings us into the next level of health and wholeness.

So what is ill health in relation to the soul? What does wholeness mean as far as the soul is concerned? What does a saved soul look like? If the pilgrim's journey is moving toward salvation, toward the health and wholeness of the soul, then what is the real goal of the pilgrim's journey?

The Soul

The Greek word for soul is *psyche*. It comes into English in the word psychology. A psychologist is one who studies the behavior of men and of animals. The mention of behavior draws attention to the reason for our interest in the psyche (soul). The behavior mechanism (the soul) is responsible for processing information and making decisions. The psyche translates our thoughts and feelings (conscious and unconscious) into action. Our soul is responsible for our cover-up actions, our exposure actions as well as the acts that express the divine nature.

The saved soul is one that has been delivered from the bondage of its unhealthy appetites, deceptive thought patterns and improper emotional responses. *A soul can freely function under God to the degree that it is free from the controlling impulses of the false self.*

Our aim as sons and daughters of God is to put off the old self which is corrupt through deceitful lusts (Ephesians 4:22). That is the *negative aspect of the salvation* (*sozo*-healing) of the soul. We must be free from the bondages (habits) of the psyche before we can hope to mature in Christ. We need liberation from the energies that drive us to continue the pretense of cover-up and from the continual inner striving for that which is empty and unfulfilling. Healing of the soul also includes giving up the need to expose our bad self-image to see if someone loves us the way we are.

The *positive aspect of the salvation* of the soul is putting on compassion, kindness, lowliness, meekness and patience (Colossians 3:12). These virtues are more than inner feelings; they are ways of manifesting the reality of who we are in Christ. Authentic spiritual growth includes the development of these attitudes and responses. We are transformed into His likeness as these qualities increase and our way of approaching and responding to others improves. The salvation of the soul is the process of coming into a state of inner health and wholeness thus increasing our ability to respond to the Holy Spirit as we lovingly relate to those around us.

This understanding of salvation as a process of *sozo* healing into wholeness allows us to understand Paul's three categories of people: 1) soulish, 2) fleshly, and 3) spiritual, found in I Corinthians 2:14-3:3. We can view each of these three classes of people from one of two different perspectives: 1) position or 2) walk (see Fig. #5).

One is *positioned* either in Christ or in Adam (I Corinthians 15:22; Romans 5:12-21). And there are only two ways of walking. One is either *walking* according to the flesh or he is walking according to the Spirit (Galatians 5:16-26; Romans 8:5-8).

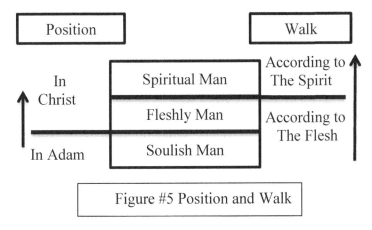

Figure #5 Position and Walk

Two Possible Positions

The false, soulish man (the Greek is *psychic*) is one whose basic source of behavior is his own psyche, his ego. He "does not accept the things of the Spirit of God, for they are folly to him, and he is not able to understand them because they are spiritually understood" (I Corinthians 2:14). Paul uses this word to describe one who is under the domination of the soul apart from and in opposition to the Spirit. In that context the soulish man is full of dishonor, corruption and weakness. He is of the earth and bears the image of the first Adam in his "fallen"

127

condition (I Corinthians 15:42-48).

Jude describes the soulish man as being devoid of the Spirit (Jude 19). It is not enough for the soulish man to wash himself and dress himself with religious deeds. In Paul's thinking, to be positioned in Adam is to be without God and without hope in this world (Ephesians 2:12). One must be born anew to move from that old position to being in Christ. He must die with Christ, be buried with Him and be raised with Him to walk in newness of life in Christ Jesus (Romans 6:4).

When we enter this new position we become a new creation. "The old [false] has passed away; behold, the new [true] has come" (II Corinthians 5:17). In this experience the Father "delivered us from the domain of darkness and transferred us to the kingdom of his beloved Son" (Colossians 3:13). We are "justified by his grace as a gift" (Romans 3:23-24). We who were enemies have been reconciled to God in Christ (II Corinthians 5:18). All this is accomplished by the grace of God apart from any human work. It is a gift of God (Ephesians 2:8-9).

Our position is altered radically when we are begotten of God and become part of His family. The arrow at the left of the diagram indicates that the change takes place *as an event* - once for all. We are no longer in Adam; we are in Christ. By virtue of our being in Christ we are in a *position* of victory over soul-bondages because he has defeated the power of Sheol by his death and resurrection. This is our position in Christ whether we are aware of it or not. Growing up into salvation involves becoming aware of what is already true for us and *learning to manifest the life of Christ* who lives in us.

We are more than conquerors through Him (Romans

128

8:37). "He disarmed the principalities and powers and put them to open shame, by triumphing over them in him," (Colossians 2:15). Our position in Him includes this victory. We are seated with Him in heavenly places (Ephesians 2:6). In Him we are far above all the powers of every spiritual enemy. As the truth of this position dawns on us we begin to actually experience victory in our daily lives and to manifest our divine nature. We *become in our action what we are in our true nature*. We begin to manifest our true, original nature as those created in the image and likeness of God.

Two Possible Ways of Walking

Our Father has changed our position so that he might begin to change our walk. "For we are His craft project, created in Christ Jesus for good works, that we might walk in them," (Ephesians 2:10). Being in Christ we have that position by virtue of the creative work of our Father. He brought us into this covenant relationship by His work of grace. But His purpose goes beyond that relationship as such. His intention is that we grow into a *full manifestation* of the salvation (wholeness) we already have in Him. That involves living our daily life according to who we are in Christ. Our new life is a daily experience of "Emmanuel, God with us." God is with us because Christ is in us. Now through us He can become Emmanuel manifest to the world around us.

Father created us for good works and He prepared good works for us to accomplish. But the good works He prepared for us are not deeds we are able to accomplish apart from the continuing working of Emmanuel, Christ in us. The works are the manifestation of the renewed relationship we have with God. *What He requires of us He works in us and through us.*

There are two different ways of "doing life" for those whose position has been altered, i.e., there are two ways of walking. There is the fleshly man who is a babe in Christ (I Corinthians 3:1) and there is the spiritual man who "discerns all things, but is himself understood by no one" (I Corinthians 2:15). Paul listed envy, strife and division as evidence that a person is walking as a babe in Christ. The "babe" is in Christ *but he does not yet act like Christ.* He does not yet demonstrate the life of Christ in his attitude and action. *He is growing toward his destiny.*

The Fleshly Man

The source of envy, strife and division is the self-will of one who has not yet adopted the mind of Christ in his way of relating to others. *Self-will and self-exaltation are infirmities in the soul* of the fleshly Christian. These infirmities hinder him from manifesting the life of the Spirit. He has not yet put off the old man; he has not died to himself. He has not yet slipped into his new identity. His soul (his behavior mechanism) is in need of *sozo* healing of these infirmities.

Paul said to the babes in Christ, "You are still of the flesh, for while there is jealousy and strife among you, you are behaving only in a human way" (I Corinthians 3:1-3). An outsider is not able to tell by the babe's *behavior* that he is in Christ. The babe has a position but does not walk the way Jesus walks. A baby in the family who has not yet learned to walk does not cease to be a member of the family. Coming to maturity in Christ as spiritual men and women is a life-long process of receiving with meekness the implanted word and allowing that living word to have its saving (*sozo*-healing) effect within the soul. The arrow at the right of the chart indicates that continuing process.

The Spiritual Man

The spiritual man is one whose soul has been healed to the point of being able to live the life of true righteousness and holiness we spoke of earlier. This ability continues to develop as long as we live. Paul recognized his need to continue to grow into the fullness. "Brothers, I do not consider that I have made it my own. But one thing I do: forgetting what lies behind and leaning forward to what lies ahead, I press on toward the goal for the prize of the upward call of God in Christ Jesus" (Philippians 3:13-14). He is not talking about going to heaven; he is talking about increasing in his ability to demonstrate God's love to the world by his life.

If we see maturity as a state of sanctification into which we should enter quickly or easily, our life will be filled with frustration or pretense and cover-up. If we try we will either live in continual self-condemnation or as mere actors in a play with no relation to reality. We will either be depressed or we will live in denial. But when we recognize sanctification as a process of becoming in our *walk* what we already are in our *position* then each new day we will be "transformed into the same image from one degree of glory to another," (II Corinthians 3:18).

131

Moving Toward the Goal

How do we advance toward the goal? How do we receive with meekness the implanted word? How do we move into a new level of wholeness? I can personally testify that it is not enough to diligently apply the natural mind to the Scripture. I have "been there, done that." There is value in Bible study and memorizing Scripture but it will never accomplish the goal if that is *all* we do. Like the initial justification it is "not because of deeds done by us in righteousness" (Titus 3:5). It is not something our natural mind and will power can accomplish.

Paul's question to the Galatians is relevant here. "Are you so foolish? Having begun by the Spirit, are you now coming to maturity by the flesh?" (Galatians 3:3). As we came to our new position by the operation of the Spirit we must also come to maturity in our walk by a work of the same Spirit (Galatians 5:25). The natural man is neither equipped nor called to accomplish any spiritual goal. He is only called to allow the Spirit to do His work in him.

Putting off the old nature must not – indeed it cannot be a work of the flesh. "But if by the Spirit you put to death the deeds of the body you will live" (Romans 8:13). Jesus said, "It is the Spirit who gives life; the flesh is no help at all. The words that I have spoken to you are spirit and life" (John 6:63). The soul cannot redeem itself nor can it heal itself of being self-centered. Coming into health and wholeness must be a work of the Spirit as we yield to His promptings. That which is flesh is flesh and can only produce more flesh.

We received Christ by believing the word of

132

justification. In the same way we mature in Christ by believing the word of *sozo* healing. As babes in Christ we long for the word-milk by which we grow into the health and wholeness of maturity. Our ability to walk as Jesus walked grows and develops as we allow the word activated by the Spirit to do its work in us. Study and memorization of Bible verses will not in itself manifest the new man. Study can be a work of the false nature trying to copycat a spiritual life to cover impurities.

Two Ways of Seeing Scripture

Our way of approaching Scripture determines what we will receive while reading. The Bible itself tells us there are two ways of reading Scripture. A quick look at Figure #6 shows that both the Old and the New Covenants have a written form. The old was written on stone (and later on paper with ink) and the new also has a written form. But the reality of the New Covenant is also written by the Spirit on human hearts (II Corinthians 3:3). The new covenant is "not of the letter, but of the spirit. For the letter kills, but the Spirit gives life" (II Corinthians 3:6). The ministry of the old brings death and the ministry of the new brings life.

The first covenant has a passing glory seen on the face of Moses. That glory faded. The second comes with a glory that endures and even increases. In the covenant written on stone, there is a veil that separates men from God. The new covenant is written on the heart and the veil is removed so we can see the glory of God with unveiled face. This inner veil that clouds our vision of God's goodness must be removed before we can receive

133

with meekness the implanted word while reading Scripture or listening to sermons. As long as we read with the veil of the flesh covering our mind we are on our own to interpret it with our intellectual and logical ability. We have words telling us about the glory but we have no experience of that glory.

Old Covenant	New Covenant
Written with Ink	Written by the Spirit
On Stone Tablets	On the Heart
Results in Death	Results in Life
Fading Glory	Enduring Glory
Veil of Separation	Unveiled Face

Figure #6 Life and Death

The Significance of the Veil

Paul presents Moses as putting the veil over his face so that the Israelites might not gaze at the full manifestation of the fading splendor (II Corinthians 3:13). In Exodus 34 it is clear that the people demanded the veil. They were threatened by the light of the glory of God on Moses' face. That is the normal response of the false soulish man to the glory of God. The unspiritual man will find many ways to veil himself from the glory even while claiming to desire it.

134

In Paul's day the Pharisees were disciples of Moses, disciples of the written code. They were convinced they knew what Scripture taught better than Paul and even better than Jesus. The apostle connected the veil over Moses' face to the hardness of the people's minds when they refused to look upon the glory of the Lord reflected in the Old Testament Scripture. *A hardened mind is one that is convinced it knows the truth simply because it knows some words that talk about truth.*

The entire saga of Mount Sinai was in the back of Paul's mind when he wrote to the believers in Corinth. In Exodus 19 and 20 the hardness resident in the hearts of the Israelites was exposed when they said to Moses, "You speak to us, and we will listen; but let not God speak to us, lest we die" (20:19). God had just promised that they would be a special people if they would hearken to his voice (19:5) and he had spoken the Ten Commandments by his voice from the mountain (20:1). They did not want a personal encounter with a speaking God. They wanted Moses to encounter God for them. Today there are many who want a pastor to encounter God for them.

We have the same situation when Moses came down from the mountain with a shining face and the Ten Commandments written on stone (*no longer a voice*). Even encountering the presence of God through the splendor on Moses' face was too much for the Israelites. Once again they recoiled at the prospect of meeting God personally. The light of God's presence exposes the flesh. Those who do not want to have their deeds exposed always flee from the light (John 3:18). Only those who know they need light will rejoice when light comes.

It is easy enough for the flesh to look at a scroll or a

135

book. Even if it is a holy book one can read it and find a way to excuse himself or deny its truth and cover his eyes from the truth it reveals. That is what I was doing while reading Pat Boone's book, *A New Song*. One might even convince himself that he is abiding by the principles in the written code as long as the only challenge comes from other men who are no better than he is. Each man interprets the text for himself and is convinced he is right and others are wrong. We all think we're right.

I have been through this many times on my journey. I have been so convinced of the truth of my doctrinal position that I would not listen to any conflicting argument – until something happened or someone said something that broke the spell off my thinking. If we are not open to hear a word contrary to what we already think we are exposed as self-righteous Pharisees.

When one comes face to face with the glory of God he is exposed, undone and without excuse. That happens even if the glory comes in a reflected form as in Moses' face. It is no wonder religious men prefer a written code to the presence of God. They can parade their righteousness or their superior knowledge before men and intimidate any who question their superior understanding. There will always be a veil separating such people from the real presence of the real God.

The New Testament had not been written at that time when Paul wrote Second Corinthians. The only Bible available to the early Church was the Old Testament. Jesus was speaking of the Old Testament when He said "it is they that bear witness about me" (John 5:39). Paul's warning about the danger of reading with a veil is valid for the reading of the New as well as the Old Testament.

136

Even in the Church there are disciples of the written text of the New Testament who avoid a personal encounter with the Author of the text and criticize those who have had an experience.

The difficulty is not in the text itself but with the hardness of the human heart which refuses to open itself to the light of the glory of God. Jesus asked the Pharisees, "How can you believe, when you receive glory from one another and do not seek the glory that comes from the only God?" (John 5:44). When we try to receive affirmation (glory) from other people who are impressed with our knowledge, performance or possessions we are exposed as those who cannot really believe. That was my condition while I was under the influence of the intellectual spirit. I was looking for affirmation from men. That is what Jesus meant when he said to me, "Fount, you haven't been believing Me, have you?" True faith comes from a personal encounter with God.

Many in Paul's day were reading the Scripture in a way that left them totally unaware of the glory of the Lord that was reflected in the text. We must be alert to the fact that it is also possible for us to read the New Testament with a veil over our minds. We can read it as a written code and see nothing but rules, regulations, doctrinal statements or simply nonsense. But the life of the resurrected and glorified Lord is missing in that. The veil must be removed. The hard heart must be softened before one can meet the living and abiding Word of God.

The god of this world has "blinded the minds of the unbelievers, to keep them from seeing the light of the gospel of the glory of Christ, who is the likeness of God" (II Corinthians 4:4). The god of this world is none other than the humanistic god which challenged Adam and Eve to try to use their natural abilities to become like deity rather than simply being who they were as persons created in the image of God. We can still eat of the same tree. It does not matter whether we partake of the knowledge of evil or the knowledge of good. *It is the same tree*. Spiritual death comes when we exalt our mind; we fall out of relationship to the Source of life.

To the degree that we try to justify ourselves before God on the basis of anything we do in the strength of our humanity, to that degree we are blinded to the light of the gospel. To the degree that we try to unlock the secrets of the kingdom by human knowledge of what is good and what is evil, to that degree we are trying to lift ourselves by our boot straps to the position of a deity. The big problem is that the veil even keeps us from seeing ourselves in our folly.

Receiving with Meekness

The veil remains unlifted for many because it is only removed through Christ (II Corinthians 3:14). "When a man turns to the Lord, the veil is removed" (v. 16). It does not say "when a man turns to the Scriptures." The mysteries of God have not been permanently unveiled in the written text in a way that they are now available to the natural mind apart from the Spirit. The Pharisees and Sadducees did not see the glory reflected in the life of the man Jesus, the Word of God in flesh, in spite of the fact that they knew the Scriptures by memory.

This brings us back to our question, "How do we receive with meekness the implanted word?" Paul

138

answered that question, "And we all, with unveiled face, beholding the glory of the Lord, are being changed into the same image from one degree of glory to another. For this comes from the Lord who is the Spirit," (II Corinthians 3:18). Our unveiled face allows us to see the glory reflected in Scriptures as it was on Moses' face. *The very experience of seeing that glory plants a word in our heart that will bring sozo healing to the soul.*

Jesus was speaking of this truth when he told the parable of the sower and the four kinds of soil. He explained to the disciples that the seed is the word and the soil is the heart. Hard hearts, like the path and the stony ground, cannot receive the word-seed. Soil containing seeds of thorns and weeds from the past will also have trouble allowing the seed to produce fruit. The good soil is the heart that turns to the Lord and receives the *sozo* healing of the soul thus removing the veil over the mind.

This is a miracle. Just as the new birth is a miracle performed "from above" so the miracle of the unveiled mind is performed "from above" on those who turn to the Lord in meekness to receive by faith the implanted word-seed (not doctrines). It is a work of God's grace administered by the Lord who is the Spirit. Having begun by the Spirit it is foolish to try to continue by a work of the flesh. God's grace is not effective for those who think they can do it with their natural abilities.

This grace-work is not a once-for-all experience like the new birth. It is a daily miracle of walking by the Spirit as we are being changed into his likeness from one degree to another by the implanted word. We cannot change ourselves. He changes us as we behold His glory. The beholding is also from Him because He is the one who removes the veil. He is the one who heals blind eyes. He is the one who appears and allows Himself to be seen. We only need to yield to Him in our approach to life.

He removes the veil for those who turn away from their false self and turn to the Lord and allow Him to do the work. The veil is removed for all who lay down their pride and take their position as humble recipients. "God opposes the proud but gives grace to the humble" (James 4:6). Pride is like an umbrella that protects us from being exposed to the light of the living and active word of God. As we put down our umbrella (pride) and receive with meekness the living word of God which is able to save your soul we begin to manifest the reality of who we already are in Christ.

So what is involved in this turning? It is an inner turning of the heart to the reality of the resurrected Christ. This concept is seen clearly in the story of Mary at the empty tomb (John 20). She was looking for a dead Jesus. First she turned around and saw Jesus, but she thought He was the gardener. That was an external turning. Today a person can turn to the "historical Jesus" and see him as a good man or even as a prophet. But they miss the reality of who he really is. That turning can only see the external of who is there. This external turning can never see the reality of the Spirit.

Mary asked where He had laid her dead Jesus. When He called her name, she turned (again) and said, "Rabboni." *The second turning was a turning of her human spirit to see the reality of what she had been looking at all along.* This second turning was a result of the enlightening of the eyes of the heart (Ephesians 1:18). There is a principle that applies here. *We tend to see what we are looking for not necessarily what is really there.* As long as we are looking for a dead Jesus (one who does nothing and says nothing today) we are looking with eyes that need to be opened. Until we experience this inner turning we will never see the living Lord who is even now standing there in front of each one of us. And we will never receive the word-seed that will bring *sozo* healing to our soul.

In the next chapter we turn our attention to man's part. How can we come to experience the miracle of the removing of the veil? How can we make that inner turn? We must get ourselves in a suitable position to receive this miracle. Our focus thus far in this book has been on discovering our identity, "Who am I." Now we ask, "What would You have me to do?"

Ten: MEEKNESS AND MIRACLES

We cannot change ourselves into his likeness. We actually do not have to because we were created in his likeness. But there are some things we need to do that will allow that likeness to unfold. We do not initiate the work of grace when we position ourselves nor do we supply the energy for the change. Like Zacchaeus we can climb the tree but it is Jesus who gives the invitation. Only at His bidding can we come down and receive Him into the house of our daily life (Luke 19:5). And He bids all to come. All we can do is take our position and wait for Him to unfold what he placed in us. The wait is not in vain because He who promised is faithful to bring us into wholeness and sanctification (I Thessalonians 5:23-24).

Issues of the Heart

When I began to teach from the new understanding of the Holy Spirit's involvement in our life I noticed there was something in me that resisted or misinterpreted the Spirit's promptings. That resistance was exposed while I was reading Pat Boone's book. That experience was related to the role of the Holy Spirit and the division of soul and spirit by the living and active word. I then began to notice that many of my responses to my wife and to students was not a pure reflection of the Life of Christ in me. That realization began the next leg in my journey. Here is how it happened.

As I was preparing for a class in book of Proverbs one text captured my attention: "Keep your heart with all vigilance; for from it flow the springs of life," (Proverbs 4:23). If what happens in my life issues from what is in my heart, I need to learn how to recognize what is in there. I realized there were impurities in my heart when I saw attitudes and behavior patterns that did not reflect the goodness of God.

"There must be something in my heart that produces inappropriate behavior," I thought, "But what is it?" I saw that the only way I could respond properly to the Spirit would be to have my heart cleansed from whatever was producing those issues.

It made sense to me that the evil in the world, and in me, is a result of the imagination of the thoughts of the heart (Genesis 6:5). The word evil refers to anything that creates alienation and hampers the manifestation of peaceful, harmonious community life. Whatever images take root in our heart will manifest themselves in our relationships without our conscious intention. The heart with its images is the base from which we operate in life. Our beholding, thinking, feeling and desiring are determined by the formative word-images that rule in our heart whether we know what is in there or not. We automatically manifest what is in our heart.

If our heart is ruled by false images (lies) of reality then our feelings will be inappropriate, our thinking will be contrary to reality and our decisions will lead to vanity and striving after wind (Ecclesiastes 1:14). But if the ruling word-images of our heart are from the living and active word of God (truth) our emotional responses will be appropriate, our thinking will reflect reality and our decisions will lead to the fullness of life on the highest plane.

143

The psalmist helped me with this also. He wrote, "I have stored up your word in my heart, that I might not sin against you" (Psalm 119:11). One difficulty is that people think of sin as doing naughty things. But *the essence of sin is any act or attitude that alienates relationships.* The ability to avoid behavior that alienates us from ourselves, from God and from one another will come as we receive images in our heart through a word received from the Source of all life and reality. When Father's living truth rules in our heart He brings deliverance from the bondages that hinder godly behavior. His truth laid up in our heart produces wholeness – *sozo* healing of the soul.

Maturity does not come from having passages of Scripture memorized as we said before. It comes when the word of the Lord *is folded into the heart.* It becomes possible to "walk in a manner worthy of the Lord, fully pleasing to him, bearing fruit in every good work and increasing in the knowledge of God" (Colossians 1:10). *But that good life can only issue from a heart purified from words, images and feelings that are contrary to reality as God created it.*

The difficulty is that we assume our concept of reality reflects actual reality. The scholars call this a cognitive bias. Cognitive bias is established in our unconscious by word-images and concepts developed in childhood and later. As we mature we begin to see the fallacy in how our parents saw the world. Then we begin to receive words from other important others like scholars or influential people. These word-images become a new cognitive filter that ignores or rejects anything that does not fit into the grid of our new way of seeing life. We see the cognitive bias of others clearly (because they disagree with us) but usually our own bias is hidden from us. We all believe that the reality we see is true reality. Me too.

Dissatisfaction Invites Change

I turn to the psalmist again for insights that are helpful here (Psalm 119:9-16). He begins with the same question we have in mind, "How can a young man [*or an older man*] keep his way pure?" The psalmist had come to realize that his way of doing life apart from God doesn't work. My attempt to connect with God was not working because my cognitive bias was filtering out any evidence of the fact that I was not dumb. It was also denying the miracles in Pat Boon's book before the spell was broken. Until we recognize our need for more reality in the way we see life there will be no movement toward the next level of maturity. *Cognitive bias rules.*

This dissatisfaction is what I experienced in Japan. The unhappiness opened me up to receive the liquid love. Again in New Mexico it was frustration with my inability to touch the students with the realities of God that brought me to recognize and acknowledge my need. I was frustrated with blind religious conformity in churches that did not allow the real presence of the real God. During that struggle I penned several Tanka verses in 1982. Here are a few of them:

ONCE

Ancient aqueduct
Debris where water flowed once
Dry desolation

145

Community of the dust
Singing "Once the Water Was."

Ashes on the hearth
Once a fire was burning here
Cold and clammy place
Groups of people bundled up
Mumbling words of yester yore.

Immortal echo
Memorial of that "once"
Audible stillness
We remember the echo
The man with his message was.

A mummy expounding
Embalmed in pastoral stance
Once was anointed
Audience happy with once
Rev'ling in what used to be.

Psalm 119:9 answered the question of how to keep
our way pure, ". . . *by guarding it according to your
word*," the psalmist wrote. The word guard implies
fencing something in on all sides. We must keep our life
"hemmed in" on all sides by the living word of the living
God. This guarding of the heart is not a work of the
fleshly outward man. The psalmist continued with a cry
from his heart, "*Let me not wander from your
commandments*" (Psalm 119:10). That heart cry reveals
his understanding that it is not something he can do of
himself. He needs help from the Source of life.

It is only after we take this position of meekness that we can begin to hide God's word in our hearts. After receiving the word in this way we must continue to maintain an attitude of meekness. *"Teach me your statutes,"* the psalmist continued (Psalm 119:12). A humble person does not assume he or she knows the meaning of the statutes. The reasoning of the false self is at a loss to understand the things of God. *If you can wrap your mind around God He's smaller than your mind.* Only those who are taught by God are able to turn to the Lord for the removal of the veil (John 6:45).

These two things, the dissatisfaction with life and realizing our need for something beyond ourselves, keep us in an attitude of meekness under the word. Meekness is not to be confused with feelings of inferiority or inadequacy. That only breeds depression and despair. Meekness is remaining aware of our need for God to *work in us what He requires of us.* The gospel is the good news that God is for us and has already done the work. We only need to receive by faith what He has done. But faith is effective only if it comes by hearing a *rhema* (presently spoken) word from Him (Romans 10:17).

Having experienced his presence as liquid love in 1957 and his lordship in 1971, there were still several negative things in my life that were issuing from my heart. Our psalmist continued with insights on *how to progress from the initial experience toward maturity*. "I will meditate on your precepts and fix my eyes on your ways" (Psalm 119:15). The word '*nabat*' (translated fixing the eyes) means to look with attention. It implies a willingness to be influenced by what you see. This brings us to biblical meditation. We will discuss three meditative

147

actions: 1) Verbalizing, 2) Vitalizing and 3) Visualizing.

1. Meditation and Verbalizing

The first meditative action the psalmist mentioned was a verbalizing of the word you hear. "With my lips I declare all the rules of your mouth," he said (Psalm 119:13). Notice it is not rules written in a book but the ones coming from the mouth of God. Simply stated we must learn to say what God is *presently* saying to us, what He is ordaining for this day. "With the heart a man believes," Paul wrote, "but with his lips he confesses and so experiences *sozo* healing" (Romans 10:10). Remember: salvation is a healing of the soul. As we continue the journey to maturity *we must speak from our mouth the word we receive in our heart from His mouth*. What we continually speak from the heart begins to adjust our cognitive bias.

"A wholesome tongue is a tree of life," Solomon wrote, "but perverseness in it breaks the spirit" (Proverbs 15:4). A wholesome tongue is one that speaks from a heart which has been cleansed of false images and which has received the word of truth with meekness. As Jesus said, "Out of the abundance of the heart the mouth speaks" (Matthew 12:34). The word-images which are abounding in the heart will come out of the mouth, especially in unguarded moments. If the word from the "mouth of God" is abounding in our heart appropriate words will come from our mouth with a proper attitude even in situations that catch us by surprise.

"Death and life are in the power of the tongue" (Proberbs18:21). Those who complain and criticize have death in their hearts so death words come out as they speak. Those who rejoice in all things (not necessarily *for* all things) have life in their hearts and speak life into their environment. We can actually create a bad day by speaking negatively. Our life will manifest the images that control our way of thinking. If the ruling image of our hearts is Christ in His victory, then we will join God who is always having a good day. When we join Him in His good day by saying what He is saying we will also have a good day.

The warning, "Watch your tongue!" is appropriate here. As we learn to *observe* what our tongue is saying (even, and especially, if it is not audible) it will reveal what is in our heart. As we discover things abounding in our heart that are not right we can begin to receive the cleansing and purifying work of the Spirit. The prayer of David will become our prayer; "Create in me a clean heart, O God, and renew a right spirit within me" (Psalm 51:10). Only God can purify our heart. Only He can make things right in our spirit. But meanwhile it is our responsibility to *guard* our own heart with vigilance.

2. Meditation and Vitalizing

The second meditative action the psalmist mentioned is vitalizing. By the word 'vitalizing' I refer to the act of making the word a vital part of our life. I speak of manifesting outwardly what we hear inwardly from Father God. Our psalmist continued, "In the way of your testimonies I delight as much as in all riches" (Psalm 119:14). The testimonies of God are stories that testify to His faithfulness. *There is a "way" indicated by the*

149

stories. For example, the story of the Exodus testifies to God's faithfulness to deliver His people from bondage. Delighting in the way of this testimony leads us to trust Him when there appears to be no way out for us.

Having learned to say what God is presently saying we now begin to manifest the reality of the abundant life indicated in the testimonies of God's mighty acts. The purpose of a testimony is to create images in the hearer's heart which will instill faith and courage to act. The woman with the issue of blood had heard reports (*rhemata* or testimonies) of Jesus' miracles (Mark 5:27). The testimonies created in her an image of touching the hem of his garment. She courageously acted on the image created by the testimonies and received healing. *What she imagined when she heard the testimony was manifest as a healing and her story became a testimony to God's mighty acts.* **Her story became an episode in His story**.

The testimonies of God's mighty acts in Scripture are designed to create in us enough trust to walk in the way of those testimonies and manifest the promises implied in the stories. The act of *vitalizing* is an act of seeing what God wants to do for us and through us and proactively going toward it. It is obedience but it is not obedience to a law. It is a rising up to *BECOME* in our experience what we *ARE* in Christ Jesus. As we actively identify ourselves with the people of God in the Bible we experience our covenant relationship with the Author of the text. Vitalizing is allowing our covenant God to do for us and in us what He has done for His other covenant partners.

3. Meditation and Visualizing

150

The psalmist's next statement is about fixing his eyes on the ways of the testimonies of God (Psalm119:15). Earlier he had said he would not be put to shame because *he had fixed his eyes on, or paid respect to* God's commandments (Psalm 119:6). He was "visualizing" in his mind's eye the *implications* of the word he was hearing. This brings us to the practice of visualization as the third activity of biblical meditation.

The *intentional* practice of meditation has been ignored in many Christian communities. I say "intentional" to bring to light the fact that *we all medi*tate. Worry is meditation. It is visualizing and dwelling on all the bad things that might happen. Lusting after a woman is meditation. It is seeing the possibility of fulfilling your inordinate desire and imaginatively engaging the image in your mind. This is what God had in mind in Genesis 6:5 when he mentioned the *imaginations of the heart* being evil continually. Worry, lust and planning evil are activities of the heart. *Imaginations come to the surface in thoughts and visual images first; then they manifest in action.* The origin of all action is the images in the heart.

We were created with an imagination. It is through the imagination that the spirit-world communicates with our spirit. The dreams and visions of biblical saints are examples of God communicating with his people through the faculty of imagination. The problem is not visualizing as such. The problem is with the source of the visions that come into our hearts. Are our hearts open to reality or are we open only to what confirms our cognitive bias? *Our heart **will receive** pictures and images from **some source**.* That is the way God created us.

Intentional visualization fell into disuse in the West

151

during the Enlightenment when humanism became the ruling paradigm. It is coming back into use in our day. Yes, there are some excesses but we must work through these excesses to bring the art of biblical meditation back into its rightful place among the list of Christian disciplines. We must overcome our fear of becoming "New Age" by visualizing. The people of God were doing this long before New Age came on the scene.

*Biblical meditation is fixing the **eyes of the heart** on the **ways of God** as outlined in the **stories** of Scripture.* As the veil is removed from our hard heart the Holy Spirit begins to show us how specific stories relate to us personally. The meekness which allows the miracle of transformation is openness for God to show up and reveal himself in a new way. This might happen while we are reading the Bible, listening to a sermon, simply being still in Father's presence or even while we are driving or taking a shower. Meekness does not set restrictions on when God might show up or what he might show. Cognitive bias does set restrictions.

My first encounter with the concept of biblical mediation came while reading Joshua 1:8. God instructed Joshua, "This book of the law shall not depart out of your mouth [**verbalize**: *say It with your mouth*], but you shall meditate on it [**visualize**: *fix your eyes on the images it presents*] day and night, that you may be careful to do [**vitalize**: *make it a part of your life*] according to all that is written in it; for then you shall make your way prosperous, and then you shall have good success."

There is a relationship between what is received inwardly through meditation and what is performed outwardly. In Psalm 119 it was stated negatively, "that I

152

might not sin against you." In Joshua it is stated positively, "that you may be able to do it." In both cases the practice of meditation with speaking and visualizing is how one hides the word in his heart. The result of having the word in your heart is *the ability to become a doer of the word and thus manifest the reality of the Christ who is in you.* But you must act on what you see.

As we receive the word with meekness, hiding it in our heart through visualizing and verbalizing, we place ourselves in a position to manifest the reality of what we see in Scripture. What we see in Scripture is accurate to the degree that the veil that clouds our vision is removed from our heart-mind as we read. It is not a magic formula. As death must precede resurrection so meekness and humility must precede true biblical meditation. We cannot manipulate God into doing what we want. Anyone who tries to control God is obviously proud. Any power than can be manipulated is not the true God.

But verbalizing and visualizing must never stand alone. We must also vitalize the word so that it becomes manifest in our daily lives. Hearing the new word from Father God does not have its full effect in our lives until we *act out* the word, *delighting in and joyfully engaging in the **way** of his testimonies.* If we do not see changes in our behavior, we have not yet hidden the word of God in our heart; we have only touched the logic of the intellectual element. Jesus was a fully human being whose action was divine. So our action must issue from the Spirit or it will be less than fully human action.

I was teaching this concept in Idaho in 1979 and made the statement "We must act as though the Word of God is true even when we don't feel like it." Someone asked me later if that was not encouraging hypocrisy. "If we really believe the Bible is true," I responded, "then *it is hypocritical to act as though it is not true.*" If we are unwilling to act as though the Bible is true we expose the fact that we do not really believe in our heart-mind that it *is* true. We only believe it in our natural mind.

4. Meditation and Forgiveness

Practical applications are in order. We will look at forgiveness first. I am personally convinced that we cannot completely overcome the negative words we received from important others until we forgive those who spoke or implied words that began our downward journey. We cannot receive the full effect of the new word from our new Father until we have forgiven. Unforgiveness clouds our vision and clutters our hearts. We cannot see life from God's perspective with a cluttered heart. *Forgiveness is the beginning of God's work toward man and must be in the beginning of man's response to others – if we want to be like Him.*

The parable of forgiveness in Matthew 18 is helpful. It is a story of a king, a steward who owed him a large debt and a fellow servant who owed the steward a small debt. The steward owed 10,000 talents of silver (some say it was equal to the entire tax base of Syria in that day). The second servant owed 100 denarii (a denarius was one day's wage for a common laborer). Neither of the servants had the resources to pay his debt.

The steward asked for mercy when the king called him to account for his stewardship. (It is important to notice that he did not ask for forgiveness.) The king did

154

three things; he had compassion, released him and forgave him. When the steward left the king's presence he met his fellow servant. He took him by the throat (*the opposite of compassion*), demanded he pay (*the opposite of forgiveness*) and put him in prison (*the opposite of release*). This unwillingness to do for another what the king had done for him is the point of the story.

The king heard about the steward's unwillingness to forgive. He put the servant in the hands of the tormentor with the words, "You wicked servant." His wickedness was simply his unwillingness to do for others what the king had done for him. He would remain in this pit of Sheol until he was able to pay his debt to the king. Today many are in the torment of the pit on one level or another. That is evidenced by their inability to enter into the abundant life Father promised. My understanding of the parable is that *the steward did not **receive** the forgiveness the king offered*. One is not able to genuinely forgive others until he has first *received* forgiveness from above.

Forgiveness in this parable is more than *verbalizing*. It includes *vitalizing*. We vitalize by releasing the debtor from the prison. I believe the prison is a metaphor for the heart of the one who refuses to forgive others. We can be in the same room with someone we have not forgiven but there are bars between us. Those bars are in our heart. Merely saying the words "I forgive you" does not release us from the torment. We are still unable to manifest the abundant life. *Compassion and release* are also necessary to make the words of forgiveness effective.

Forgiveness is releasing the debtor from the **obligation** to pay. Release has to do with the **penalty** for not paying. We often penalize others by refusing to allow

155

Father's love to flow through us to them. Or we just remain bitter hoping they will get what they deserve. We want them to pay for what they did. The prison is in the heart of the one who is unforgiving. Something needs to happen in the heart, not merely in the mouth. The closing statement of the parable confirms this. "So also will my heavenly Father do to each one of you unless you forgive your brother from your heart." Father wants us to grow into his likeness by having compassion, forgiving from the heart and releasing others as he has done for us.

Practical Application: First Example

Every father owes his sons and daughters love and fatherly attention. Every mother owes her sons and daughters love and motherly comfort. These are legitimate debts. It is not unreasonable to think the father or mother owes these things if they have not done it effectively. Our parents, like the fellow servant, may not have been able to pay that debt, probably because they never received what they needed from their parents. They have 'insufficient funds' in their love account. Many people do not recognize their parent's debt because they blame themselves for not being good children, as though the reason the parents failed was their fault.

My wife and I facilitate this forgiveness by having people visualize an IOU signed by their father or mother (or whoever is a debtor). On the IOU is a list of the things the parents were not able to do for the child. You can experience the process as I relate the steps here.

Knowing that our King has forgiven your debt and released you from the obligation to pay, *visualize* yourself with the IOU in your hands with the details of what they owe. Tear up the IOU and *saying the words* "I forgive you." In this way you are meeting your debtor after receiving forgiveness from the king. The debtor does not have to be physically present. You are meeting the debtor who is internalized in their heart.

When we notice that these internal bars maintain alienation between people we become aware that there are many barriers that separate fathers from sons, sisters from brothers, mothers from children and friends from friends. We have put one another in a debtor's prison. Notice also that *the torment in our lives is not because important others failed us; it is because we have not forgiven those who failed us.* It is not what they did; it is our response to them that keeps us in torment.

We are not always consciously aware of our unforgiveness because it is below consciousness. I was ministering to a young lady who had a serious eating disorder including anorexia, bulimia and some food allergies. She was not aware that she was inwardly angry with her parents. She had blamed herself for the problem. In our time together she became aware of the hidden resentment. I led her through the forgiveness exercise described here and she was healed of her eating disorder as well as her food allergies. Her parent's negative words were a formative element in her disorder. When she forgave her parents the negative words were defeated and the disorder no longer tormented her.

First we recognize ourselves as the ones who are in the hands of the tormentor because of our unforgiveness. *We are not there because of what happened to us but because of our response to what happened.* Then we acknowledge (confess) our unforgiveness to God. This begins the process of vitalizing the word of forgiveness. Complete freedom does not come if we only forgive and tear up the IOU. We must also release the persons from our judgments. We must let them out of our inner prison.

We recommend that people see themselves in front of the jail cell where the debtor is held. You have just torn up the IOU. Now take a key, unlock the door and speak release to the debtor. You are doing this as an act of obedience to Father's word but also as an act of compassion. As the person leaves the cell speak a blessing toward them. In this act you become like your Father who forgave you your debt, released you from bondage and blessed you. This act is not for the debtor's sake; it is for your own freedom. It is between you and your King. It is an added bonus if the debtor changes. Sometimes they do and sometimes they do not. But the one who forgives is free.

Christ is there on the scene to minister to you after you have forgiven and released your debtor. We are not pretending; He is really there in our spirit! Turn to Him in your spirit and let Him balance your love-ledger by ministering Father's embrace.

Healing the Wounded Heart

One other step is helpful. If we have not been able to effectively love our parents, siblings, children etc., it is because our love account is also in the red. Our heart was broken when we did not receive love the way we needed it as a child. We will not be completely free until the wound is healed. If the wound is not healed the resentment may return when we feel the pain again.

Jesus read from Isaiah 61 when He began his ministry. The passage says He came to bind up the broken heart and set at liberty the captive. As you stand there having torn up the IOU and unlocked the prison door, ask Jesus to do what He came to do. Say, "Jesus, bind up my broken heart and set me free." Then take a moment in silence to receive healing. As Jesus does this your life will begin to be vitalized by the love of Father God.

The first time I applied this principle was with a widow's daughter. The father had died of a heart attack when she was nine years old. When the daughter was about twelve, her mother began to talk about dating so the daughter would have a father in her teen years. The daughter went ballistic. She did not want a man in the house. Both the mother and the daughter realized this reaction was excessive so they asked Lynda and me to come over. During our time together the daughter said, "I felt like my dad did not love me enough to stay." I told her to forgive her dad and invite Jesus to bind up her broken heart as in Isaiah 61. She "saw" Jesus come with a needle and thread and sew up her heart. She was free and began to urge her mother to get her a new daddy.

Practical Application: Second Example

Hebrews 12:1-16 offers another example. The text begins with an exhortation to look to Jesus, the author and finisher of our faith. The word translated 'look' refers to seeing with the heart-mind and suggests the idea of visualizing that we describe here. Then the writer encourages us to consider Him who endured hostility against Himself. The words translated 'consider' refers to an act of contemplation (meditation) which is also an act of the heart. The exhortation is to allow the behavior you observe in Jesus' life to become a way of life for you. In other words, it is calling us to *vitalize* the implications of what we see when we look to Jesus.

The purpose of this contemplation is to help us avoid becoming weary and fainthearted. It is so easy for us to become weary when others continually express hostility toward us. Usually we retreat back into our "closet" or counter their attack with hostility. A passive, fearful person might simply compromise to avoid conflict.

What do we *see* when we consider Jesus? We see a man who is at peace with God and at peace with Himself. When others attack Him or fail to show due respect it does not evoke a response of anger or uncover hidden resentments. He has no T-shirt to hide and no sin to cover. On the cross He has only compassion and forgiveness for those who are expressing the ultimate hostility against Him. *Only love flows from His wounds*. What flows from your wounds?

He did not succumb to the human tendency to sin (alienate others) by fighting back, withdrawing or compromising. "When he was reviled, he did not revile in return," Peter wrote (I Peter 2:23). This is the attitude the Hebrew writer is calling us to behold and adopt as our own. "In our struggle against a sinful response to the hostility of others," he wrote, "we have not yet resisted to the point of shedding blood" (Hebrews 12:4). Our false nature will not shed its blood to avoid returning hostility for hostility. Our false nature will defend itself even at the costs of the other's blood. The Pharisees demonstrated

160

this truth when they gave Jesus over to the Romans.

Each of us has a "boiling point" beyond which we no longer resist expressing the anger we have against those who do not honor us as we think we deserve. Those with an aggressive nature become a jailer who makes the debtor pay for his sin. Those more passive will simply hide (shut down and blame themselves) or compromise rather than shed their blood. *Shedding of blood here means laying down your self-life for the sake of maturity in Christ.*

At this point the text makes a curious turn. The apostle reminds us that God has addressed us as sons. Then he adds, "It is for discipline that we have to endure." We must endure the hostility of sinners. Father does not send hostile sinners, but he does use them to train us in righteousness, so we may share His holiness (Hebrews 12:10). This is the holiness of Jesus in his willingness to endure the hostility of sinners without reacting. It is not an abstract holiness. His holiness is His willingness to empty Himself of His divine prerogatives in order to communicate Father's love to humanity.

When we turn the other cheek we behave as Jesus did. When we go the second mile with the hostile sinner we reflect Father's love to the sinner. When we give our cloak to the one who took our coat we become like Christ in true righteousness and holiness. In short we allow our lives to be *vitalized* by the implanted word of the Father who loved us in this way. The Christ in us becomes manifest as we express His love to others.

The text continues, "For the moment all discipline seems painful rather than pleasant, but later it yields the peaceful fruit of righteousness to those who have been trained by it" (Hebrews 12:11). Peaceful fruit comes to those who receive training in difficult situations. Those who do not submit to the training will never see the joy and peace that come on the other side of suffering. Joy and peace come to those who look to Jesus who, for the joy that was set before him, endured the cross and is seated at the right hand of God (Hebrews 12:2).

The author offers one final insight in this regard. "See to it that no one fails to obtain the grace of God; that no 'root of bitterness' springs up and causes trouble" (Hebrews 12:15). The phrase 'fail to obtain' was a banking term secular Geek in New Testament times. The phrase is roughly equivalent to our phrase "insufficient funds." It means that you came up short in your grace account and your grace-check will bounce. When we encounter a hostile sinner and try to be gracious our grace fails. We end up being hostile in return, shutting down or compromising to avoid rejection.

As I was learning this I had an experience that planted this word deep in my heart. My wife was failing to give me the honor I thought I deserved. Every time I tried to be gracious I lost my cool, walked out and slammed the door. My grace account had insufficient funds to cover the conflict. When I asked Father to help me I sensed that I was writing the check on the wrong account. I did not know I had two accounts so I began to seek clarification and came to see something new.

I saw that I have an account to draw the grace I need for myself. That account is full and will never be depleted. But I also have an account to draw grace for my wife when she needs it. I had been writing the check on the account of grace for myself. Then I saw it: I was trying

162

to use my Father's grace to look good in the eyes of the students, to feel good about myself and have a spiritual advantage over Lynda. I suddenly realized how self-centered I had been and how I needed to experience another level of *sozo* healing for my soul.

In our self-centeredness we fail to recognize that the one being hostile toward us is in need of God's grace as much as we are. In our self-righteousness we ask for grace to get through the situation looking like a super saint. We want to stay calm so the hostile sinner will be exposed and others will be on our side against them. It is no wonder God withholds the grace we would use to exalt ourselves at the expense of others. God resists the proud and gives grace to the humble.

The grace Father gives in difficult situations is the grace we need to walk through the valley. But it also includes the grace he wants to offer through us to the one who drove us into the valley. If we allow this discipline (training) to move our attention away from ourselves, we will notice that the hostile sinner is in need of grace. Jesus did not merely pray that He might receive grace to endure the cross; His heart went out in compassion for the ones who were crucifying Him. He prayed, "Father forgive them, they don't know what they're doing" (Luke 23:34).

When we fix our eyes on Jesus and His way, when we delight in following him, we become doers of the word not merely hearers of the word. We begin to manifest the reality of the abundant life available in Him. As we willingly position ourselves in meekness before God and in humility before our fellowman we begin to be like the One who "did not count equality with God a thing to be grasped" (Philippians 2:4). In this way we manifest

His holiness, the holiness of His love. We manifest divine sonship. We advance from one degree of glory to another.

The word of God will become a creative element in our lives *only* as we receive it with meekness and allow it to transform our thinking, feeling and behaving. When we *receive* the new word by allowing it to change our attitude it will become a living and active word in us. It will produce the image and likeness of God in us. This takes time and is sometimes painful but it is the power of God unto salvation (*sozo healing*) for those who believe (Romans 1:16). It initiates the transformation of the mind of those who present themselves to God in meekness as a living manifestation of Father's love (Romans 12:1-2).

We have dis-covered who we are in Christ and we have seen the necessity of receiving with meekness the implanted word that will bring us to health and healing in our soul. We are almost ready to grapple with the question, "What would you have me to do."

Before we approach that question, the next chapter will focus on the danger of trying to superimpose our personal god-image over the true God, trying to get him to conform to our image.

Eleven: THE GOD WHO IS

Life is a series of transitions. For our purpose we can divide life into three major stages. The first stage is the openness of **childhood**. This phase involves several transitions as we grow physically, learn more and have a variety of experiences. The second stage we call **striving**. Life becomes more and more complex as we transition through receiving an education, finding a job and perhaps starting a family. In this stage there are the transitions of advances, setbacks in our jobs and in our relationships.

The third stage we call the **second childhood**. This comes when we have learned how to accept life as it comes and no longer try to control everything by attacking, hiding or compromising. Then we understand what Jesus meant when he said we must become as a little child. Some grow old chronologically but never come to this final stage. It is not a matter of chronology. Some learn this very early in life. But it is easy to get bogged down in either of the first two stages and fail to transition into the second childhood.

A transition is like a curve in the road. Someone said, *"A bend in the road is not the end of the road unless you fail to negotiate the curve."* When we fail to make a proper transition from one stage in life to another we face unnecessary difficulties and are frustrated in our attempt to reach the next level of development. We remain stuck in the bar ditch of life. The path does not move when we get off track. But if we do not know we are off track, we will flounder around wondering why things go wrong.

This chapter will elaborate on the significance of the

image of God we have in our heart and how that image, coupled with our self-image and our world-image, influences our lives. A brief review will help prepare us for this discussion. First we raised four basic questions. 1) Where did I come from? 2) What am I becoming or where am I going? 3) What is this world all about and how do things work? 4) What or who is my source of strength and direction? All four of these questions dovetail with the major question, *"Who am I really?"*

The fourth question is our concern here. Who (or what if we don't believe in God) is available to help me enter into the abundant life? The god of this world" (II Corinthians 4:4) is a deceiver and he is untrustworthy. And there is the One Creator and Redeemer who is the ultimate Source of all that is. This Source of life is trustworthy. Our question here is basically, *"Who am I in the power structure of life and its struggles?"*

Our images of reality effect the way we think and respond in any given situation. Our conception (image) of the world and the laws that govern life will determine our expectations and responses. For example, modern neuroscience has discovered that what we see "out there" is determined largely by what we expect to see. About 80% of what we "see" is supplied by images in our memory bank (i.e. our unconscious expectations). Since we respond according to what we believe or think is "out there," our responses will be appropriate only to the degree that we are seeing correctly.

The three basic images that affect our seeing are the self-image, the world-image and the God-image. Our focus so far has been on the self-image, how it develops and how to receive *sozo* healing. In this chapter we consider the God-image as it relates to the self-image and the world-image. We will see how these interface with each other to influence our lived lives.

The God-Image

As a preliminary definition we simply state that the God-image is our conception of who (or what) is the ultimate power or authority that influences the direction and success of life. To make the point in the form of a question we ask, "To what (or to whom) must we render ultimate respect and honor? From whom (or from what) can we expect a good life? Who (or what) can we trust with our lives?" Stating the issue in this way illuminates the importance of the God-image. This ultimate respect is what we call worship. Atheists have rejected an image of God, not necessarily the real God. When someone says, "It's all about the bottom line," his source of security and significance is money, his god. During my college days my intellect became my god because I thought it was my source of security and significance.

While I was a student at the University of New Mexico I was on the intramural wrestling team. Unconsciously I saw myself as a loser. I saw my opponent as bigger, stronger and more experienced. That was my world-image. God was not even an issue because in my mind He was only there on Sunday and was only interested in what happened in the church building. That limited God-image left me to my own resources to fight the battle. I actually had more respect and honor for my opponent than I did for the god of my imagination.

With "li'l ole' me" coming up against that huge giant

167

of a man and with an "unavailable god," who could expect me to win? It is as though I saw life as a series of contests in which I was to play the role of the loser. My place in the world was to provide someone for all those winners to defeat. My image of God was of no value in life as I lived it at that time. (The amazing thing is that Father God was with me in spite of my weak God-image.)

The first thing wrong with this image is that my fellow wrestler and I were both the same weight. Actually I was probably stronger than he because I was working out on weights with a trainer. The second thing wrong, which I learned later, is that he was also fighting his first match. We both had the same level of experience. He was an experienced giant only in my imagination. But when the opportunity came for me to gain the advantage I hesitated and lost the match. I was defeated by my imagination before I took my place on the mat.

Another example is my experience with weightlifting. My trainer wanted me to enter the annual New Mexico weightlifting competition. I saw myself (self-image) as the "ninety-eight-pound weakling" whose picture I saw in barbell advertisements. I knew all the other contestants would be huge, barrel-chested men with the classical physique of the Greek gods. I could see myself on stage dropping the bar and the audience laughing as my opponent came to lift with one arm what I had dropped. The laughing crowd and the strong opponent were from the negative words my dad spoke.

I gave my trainer some silly excuse saying I could not enter the contest, but I did attend the as a spectator. To my amazement the young man who got first place in my weight class won it with about three pounds less than

I could lift. Actually I may not have won the contest even if I had entered. Images have a way of influencing behavior and proving themselves to be true. I would have found a way to lose the contest and still appear (at least to myself) to be doing my best. I had to fulfill my self-image as a loser with an unavailable god.

The point here is that I was defeated by the interplay of my self-image, my world-image and my image of a god who was not available outside the church building. A person with a more aggressive nature who thinks of himself as weak may put forth greater effort to overcome his weakness. He might win the contest even though he does not believe in God at all.

Words Create Images

You will recall that the images are related to the words we receive from important others in our formative years. Sometimes the words were never stated out loud. They were only implied by our *interpretation* of the meaning of events or circumstances. Once I had received the image of the "Dumb-Dumb-Loser" I could not accept any evidence to the contrary. With an image of the world as hostile all I could see was giants and walled cities.

Whatever may actually be out there in the real world, *we view our personal world through the images we receive through words **about** the world.* We see what we expect to see and we expect to see what the words we received have prepared us to see. For example, if a boy received a word that young unmarried girls are fun and married women (his mom) are hostile he will probably see hostility in his wife even when she is kind and gentle.

He did not see hostility in her before they were married because she was not yet a married woman.

The "unmarried-girls-are-fun" image might then kick in after he is married. When he gets tired of his wife's continual resistance (even if it is only in his imagination) he would see young unmarried girls as more desirable than this wife and he would see opportunities to have fun. If he divorced his wife and remarried, he would likely begin to see his new wife just as hostile as the one he divorced. That is the power of the images in the heart.

The word received in childhood can only be replaced by a new word from a source strong enough to overpower the old word and capture the imagination. In the above example there was no God-image strong enough to guard the man's heart from lust. The false images influenced his attitude and behavior toward his wife. The extent and value of any change will depend on the source of the new word. There are many potential sources: society, the church group and professors just to name a few. A preacher's word will not carry power to change the heart unless God is speaking through him.

Even if the new word comes from God its effect will depend on the level of trust. With a "god-who-is-never-there" it would be difficult to trust the new word even if it is from the true God. The lack of trust in the authority or power of the person who gives the new word will limit that word's ability to make permanent changes in the heart. Outward behavior may change to conform to the new perception but the changes will be superficial.

The True God is the only source that can affect fundamental changes in our hearts. *The image of God in our minds is not God*; it is only an image and may be imaginary. The influence of the True God apart from trust in His real presence will be limited. The word of God comes with the power of God for those who hear Him speak His word into their heart. We experience the reality of the living and active word as we receive it with meekness, as we *take our position in the bosom of the Father under the authority of the word He is speaking.*

When with the "ears of our heart" we hear Him say we are "more than conquerors through him who loved us" (Romans 8:37), we can *receive* that word and *speak* it in faith. In this way we enter the process of allowing the Conqueror in us to manifest Himself in our experience. As we learn to say in faith, "I am what God says I am in this world," we can begin to act as though that is really true (because it is true). Our self-image and our world-image begin to take shape according to the word of God when we fix our eyes on that word, receive it in our heart and speak it with our mouth. *We are changed into the likeness of Him who has conquered death. We enter into the resurrected life with Him at the same time.*

The God Who Is

Returning to the matter at hand concerning the image of God we raise the question, "What if I had approached my opponent in the wrestling contests with a different concept of God?" Suppose I had entered that wrestling match with an image of God as one who would never let me lose. I might have gone farther with that image than I did with the one I had. Sooner or later there would have been another wrestler who believed God would not allow him to lose. If I had won that match should I conclude that

171

God loves me more than my opponent? If I lost would that mean God had abandoned me?

Those questions lead into a blind alley. *The God who takes sides with particular families, nations or groups does not exist except in the imagination of the people in those groups.* Is that biblical? The Old Testament God is in fact the God of Israel. But he is also God over all nations as well. The story of Joshua makes it clear that God was willing to take sides with Israel's enemies. This complicates the issue for those who want a God they can keep in a box, one who takes care of them and never lets trouble enter their lives. That is a no-god, a figment of the imagination of self-centered people and people groups.

I will illustrate from the Bible what I mean.

Consider Joshua 5:13-15. Joshua was walking near Jericho at night after leading the people across the Jordan River in obedient response to God's instructions. He was probably considering possible battle plans. Suddenly there was a man standing before him with a drawn sword in His hand. Like any good military man Joshua immediately challenged Him and demanded He identify Himself.

"Are you for us or for our adversaries?" Joshua demanded. With this question the battle line was clearly drawn. If the man was on Israel's side Joshua could relax. But if the man was for the people of Jericho Joshua had a conflict on his hands.

The man's answer came with profound implications. "No, but as commander of the army of the Lord I have now come." A paraphrase of his answer will catch its significance. "Joshua, *I did not come to take sides. I came to take over.* I have not come to honor the battle lines you

172

have drawn. I have come as Lord. Whether I am on your side or not depends on your response to My lordship. Take off your shoes in My holy presence" (Joshua 5:15).

The Lord proceeded to outline an odd battle plan (Joshua 6). Joshua and his army executed the plan by marching around the city one time each day for six days. On the seventh day they circled the city seven times, blew their shofars and shouted a victory cry. The walls of Jericho fell and Israel experienced a great victory.

This story is not about a man or a group manifesting faith. *It was God manifesting His faithfulness.* The victory was not a result of Joshua's ability to capture the imagination of his troops with an idea of what God *might* do. The power of positive thinking, valuable though it may be, does not cause walls of stone fourteen feet thick to crumble and fall. The true God made His lordship known in that event and proved Himself to be in charge of His creation.

YaHWeH (Jehovah), the God of Israel, was not formed in the people's imagination by the preaching of a charismatic leader. YaHWeH is not a creation of man's imagination. He created man with an imagination; man's imagination did not create Him. Men often carve images in wood or stone to match the image of God they have in their mind. Israel's God did not allow Himself to be restricted by an image fashioned by man. Jeremiah said those man-carved gods are "worthless things in which there is not profit. Can a man make for himself gods?" Then he added, "Such are no gods," (Jeremiah 16:19-20).

A False Image

The next story in the book of Joshua demonstrates the futility of following a concept of God. The people wanted to go up against the next city, Ai. It was a smaller city and less fortified. *The image of God that formed in the people's minds was based on the actual events of the crossing of Jordan and the crumbling walls of Jericho.* But the battle they were about to fight was not preceded by instruction from the Captain of the Hosts. They made their plan based on an idea in the people's minds. They did not carve this image in stone but it was none the less a no-god, an image in their mind with no ultimate power.

"Do not have all the people go up," they suggested, "but let about two or three thousand men go up and attack Ai" (Joshua 7:3). The world-image operating here is: "those few little insignificant people up there in that li'l ole' city." The God-image and self-image influencing their thinking was: "Our God can tear down stone walls. *With a God like that on our side we can conquer this small city with very little effort.*"

The thinking of the men was logical enough. And it was even based on an act of the real God. They were able to capture the imagination of the troops with no trouble. The God who delivered Jericho into their hands with such a display of power would have no trouble conquering Ai. But the people were running forward with the assumption that the God who was with them against Jericho would *automatically* be with them against Ai.

When they launched the attack the image of "God-with-us-no-matter-what" was highly charged and even had apparent historical confirmation. But it was not strong enough to defeat "li'l ole Ai" since God himself was not with them. This incident opened Joshua up to

174

receive the next level of revelation of the nature of the Commander of the Lord's army. Joshua had not fully processed the truth of His lordship.

After this defeat Joshua prayed, "Alas, O Lord YaHWeH, why have you brought this people over the Jordan at all, to give us into the hands of the Amorites, to destroy us?" (Joshua 7:7). Even Joshua was assuming YaHWeH would be with them. The Lord's response was essentially, "It is not time to pray; it is time to pay attention to the Commander." Our point is that *if you want to be involved in the kingdom of God you must abandon your personal image of God and how He operates.*

This shows us something about the Commander's response to Joshua in his original encounter. *God's commitment to man is never a blank check.* He does not make Himself or His resources available to defend the battle lines as we draw them. In our day whole villages of Muslims are receiving dreams from the Lord and becoming Christian. This is evidence that *this God does not take sides against the "heathen."* There are also Christian groups that are experiencing the absence of God in their difficult situations. The true God is trying to get our attention. He wants to bring us to reality.

The plan of attack against Ai was under the influence of a false image of God. A *false image is a false god.* The people were following their own human logic rather than the man who held the drawn sword. God has not obligated Himself to act on our ideas of what He ought to do. In the religious cultures of that day each tribe believed that their tribal god was on their side. Israel believed the same thing. That set them up for disillusionment.

The name by which He identified Himself to Moses

was "I AM WHO I AM," or, as the margin has it, "I WILL BE WHAT I WILL BE" (Exodus 3:14). This name comes into English in the transliteration, YaHWeH or Jehovah. This name flew in the face of the cultural understanding of God. People in that culture thought one could influence their god's activity if he knew the right name and how to pronounce it. But the True God reserves the right to express Himself in whatever way He chooses in any given situation. By this name YaHWeH God made it clear that Moses would not be able to manipulate Him to do what Moses or the people wanted Him to do.

The Danger of False Images

At some point in our early lives we receive words about God that formed an image in our heart-mind. *God created man to respond to words* because he planned to influence men and women by His Word. We were created to receive our self-image, our world-image and our God-image through spoken and enacted words of important others. We receive these formative words at an age when we do not yet question. As we receive those words with meekness (without resistance) the words become a major influence in our thoughts, emotions and behavior.

Since the beginning of time the words children receive are words of men and women whose images are not completely accurate. They are the words of man *about* God rather than the words of God. As long as the God-image is only tested in a community where everyone believes the same things the child develops his concept of God within the confines of the deluded community. One may remain faithful to the delusion even unto death if he is never exposed to anything beyond his little community.

The God-Who-IS has ways of using crisis situations to challenge us to choose between Him and our images as He did with Joshua. By the time we reach mid-life most of us have discovered that our childhood *image* of God cannot save us or give us abundant life. Our concepts are worthless and empty even if they are based on something God actually did. We can only expect frustration when our God-image is actually a no-god. We come to a crossroad in our journey when the no-god disappoints us. We must decide which road we will follow from there.

One road leads to atheism. "Since my god has not proven himself to be real there must be no God." Many have followed this path. Bertrand Russell is one example. In 1963 I read an article he wrote called, "Why I Am Not a Christian." As I read that article I could not help but think, "If God were as he described him, I would be an atheist as well." The god he described was one of the no-gods created by a legalistic religious spirit. The Christ he rejected was one of the many antichrists who have come into the world (I John 2:18). *One does not dispose of the True God when he rejects a false god.*

The second road one might choose leads to the religiosity against which Bertrand Russell spoke. When the true God does not do things our way we can deny the reality or significance of the crisis and exalt the god of our imagination. This is common in a community where the members are required to believe the Church doctrines in spite of confusion or evidence to the contrary. *These communities use the fear of rejection (the power of Sheol) to control the people.* The concern about the community's reaction may have value in certain circumstances but not

177

when the True God is trying to get our attention. This denial of reality can develop in a variety of ways.

To save our God-image we might build a strong political structure within our churches to enforce the rules of our no-god. These rules are enforced by the ultimate sanction: excommunication from the in-group of the "people of God." In the church I grew up in the preachers convinced us that others were deluded if they claim to have life from God in a way inconsistent with our image. "After all," they told us, "they cannot really be receiving from God since they are not part of our group."

By mental gymnastics we also formulate doctrines to defend our no-god from the logical attacks of those who do not believe what we believe. When they present evidence of God's favor in their own experience we hide behind our doctrinal walls and political structures. We comfort ourselves with the thought that although they may be receiving blessings in this life we will have greater blessings in the life to come. We go blindly through life clinging to our no-god. It works well as long as we remain behind the walls of our doctrinal fortress.

Some are able to amass great wealth and to have a good life with their assertive attitude and behavior. They may use their success in life to insist that their image of God is true. If they are atheists, they use their success to prove there is no God. But there are resources and powers available to humans that can work wonders apart from the guidance of the Holy Spirit. And those powers aren't demonic, they are human powers. For example, the "power of positive thinking" is a power available apart from divine intervention. That power is related to the true God because He created man with that ability. To the degree that a man's imagination is influenced by the living Word of the living God, only to that degree his actions will be authentically spiritual.

When we set ourselves to a task with sufficient aggressiveness we might be able to "prove" that God is with us when it is really a no-god that is with us. We may gain enough influence to dominate others and use our political influence as evidence that God is on our side. Then we begin to produce logical and systematic arguments that support what we already believed before any evidence was available. Even a ministry of signs and wonders is not proof that the true God is with us. Jesus says to those who prophesied, cast out demons and worked miracles, "I never knew you; depart from me, you workers of lawlessness," (Matthew 7:23).

If we have a god who will support our false-self and fulfill our self-centered vision, it is not the God who allowed the Israelite army to experience defeat at Ai. A god who is impressed with our human wisdom and who needs our logical defense is not the God who uses the foolish things of the world to shame the wise (I Corinthians 1:27). Many intellectuals are objectively shamed even though they are honored by society and *feel* no shame.

The third alternative at the crossroad of crisis is a road which few are willing to travel. It is a way which allows the true God to manifest himself as the God He IS without any need of human direction, definition or defense. This way allows God to choose how He will express His divinity in each situation. On this road man takes a position in crisis that can say concerning his false god, "If he [Baal] is god, let him contend for himself, because his altar has been torn down" (Judges 6:31).

This puts us in a vulnerable position if we are trying to establish ourselves in this world as men or women of significance. *It takes more real faith to allow God to prove Himself over against our image than it does to take a firm position with the god we created in our imagination.* We are vulnerable because there is no guarantee that God will manifest Himself in a way that will prove our image of Him is correct. The true God models this: He allows himself to appear powerless.

Even if we have represented Him accurately, His act might take a form which others do not *recognize* as an act of God. True faith leaves our humanity in a vulnerable position. Even Jesus was vulnerable in this way. The religious people rejected Him as a blasphemer. On the Cross He appeared powerless. By allowing our humanity to remain vulnerable we allow God to prove Himself in His own way. "Therefore I will boast all the more gladly of my weaknesses," Paul wrote, "so that the power of Christ may rest upon me" (II Corinthians 12:9).

Mental Idolatry

Images of God carved in stone are idols. The true God is alive and active. And He does not live in a box. He is free. We all understand this as a true doctrine but we often fail to realize that images in our mind can be as idolatrous as the ones in stone. The images in our mind become idols and cloud our vision of the true God when we expect Him to behave according to our cognitive bias.

The false images also cloud the vision of who we are. Many of our frustrations are a direct result of these

180

inappropriate images. We find ourselves in difficult situations when we expect God and the world to conform to our image. We try to adjust our behavior according to what we *think* God and the world expect of us in the role we have chosen in life. We are surprised when neither God nor the world responds as we think they should. This defeats our attempt to manifest the abundant life. Our false god is tried and found to be an anemic, powerless warped idea of the true God. Though he makes sense in our heads and sounds good in our self-talk, he is a false god and only exists in the little box of our mind.

We try to live according to what we *imagine* God expects of us and we are devastated when He does not hold up His end of our bargain, *a bargain He never agreed to.* When we try to force God and the world into a mold of conformity to our images things go haywire and we either blame God or deny His existence. Things get worse and we wonder why. We seldom stop to consider that the true God is trying to get our attention. Things will not improve until we humble ourselves in meekness under the Living Word of the Living God.

If we would be more sensitive to the true God our lives would be less complicated, not necessarily less difficult. There would still be struggles but we would be less anxious because the *definition of success and the burden of success would be on His shoulders instead of ours.* Our conflicts would be with unreality, with the lie and the Liar, rather than with Him or with other people. And we would fight those battles in the power of His might instead of in our own strength. Where might we end up in this journey if we could learn to *follow* the God who IS rather than trying to *lead* Him?

Isaiah noticed, "Bel bows down; Nebo stoops; their idols are on beasts and livestock; these things you carry are borne as burdens on weary beasts." He continued, "Listen to me, O house of Jacob, all the remnant of the house of Israel, who have been borne by me from your birth, carried from the womb; even to your old age I am He, and to gray hairs I will carry you. I have made, and I will bear; I will carry and will save" (Isaiah 46:1-4).

We try to carry God instead of allowing Him to carry us. "I do not want to let God down," we say – *as though we are the one holding Him up*. We try to save our idea of God (Bel) rather than allowing Him to save us. We carry the burden of the world because we do not trust God to carry it. We stoop under the pressure. All this is because our image is an idol, a no-god.

So in summary, we begin life trying to find what we can do that will make us significant. We try to answer the question of a helper in life by entering into various relationships, including a relationship with a "higher power." And we try to solve the problem of support by entering the world of business or service. All these activities are necessary and good but they become a problem when we exalt them to a place of a god.

In his book *The Four Loves* C. S. Lewis realized that, if we make Eros a god, it becomes a demon. That principle applies when we make anything a god, whether it be our intellect, our possessions or our position.

When we move to the final stages of life we begin to see things differently. Most of all we begin to see ourselves differently. *God has not changed; we have.*

Twelve: I AM . . . AT REST

Returning Forward

T. S. Elliot said it well in *The Four Quarters*:

"What we call the beginning is often the end
And to make an end is to make a beginning."

My great nephew, Tanner Clark (age 7), realized something at a young age:

His Grandmother: "Tanner, why are you sad?"
Tanner: "I'm sad because my childhood is almost over and I really like being a kid."

In psalm 131: 1-2 David personally experienced the final stage of life as a beginning of something new. He wrote: "O Lord, my heart is not lifted up; my eyes are not raised too high; I do not occupy myself with things too great and too marvelous for me. But I have calmed and quieted my soul, like a nursed child with his mother; like a nursed child is my heart within me." This was the beginning of David's new way of being. This is the second childhood.

The heart of a young man is generally lifted up and his eyes are raised high. Mine was – once I woke up from my bad dream of being a Dumb-Dumb failure. Youth expects to accomplish something great. Sometimes we do, but having attained great things we are often not as satisfied as we thought we would to be. Our heart feels empty when we are alone with ourselves and our trophies. When we *overcome our need to be identified by our achievements, positions and possessions* we can leave anxious toil behind and enter into rest like a child at his mother's breast.

After a life of striving to be an individual with a reputation, one who stands out as a Bible teacher and scholar, my heart is no longer lifted up, no longer struggling to be special in the eyes of others. I have finally come to rest in simply being in-and-of the One who IS. That is apparently what David experienced above in Psalm 131. His heart was more like a child in his mother's arms than like a striving adult at that point in his life. *When we return to childhood we are returning forward* not backwards. Allow me to unfold this statement.

More than once Jesus put a child in front of the disciples as an example of readiness to receive. "Truly I say to you, unless you turn back and become as children, you will never enter the kingdom of heaven," He said (Matthew: 18:3). His point was that the only ones who can recognize and be ready for what Father has to offer are those who have the heart of a child. This "turning back" is actually a turning forward toward a new future of becoming child-like as adults. This is what we are calling the second childhood.

There are many smaller and larger transitions in life as we have noticed. There are seasons of blessing and seasons of struggle. Each struggle is preparation for the next stage of life, like a butterfly coming out of the chrysalis. These are thresholds we must cross as we come out of what we have been into what we are becoming. We are returning to a beginning place but we are moving

184

forward. As it turns out the new place is another doorway of transition into what we will be tomorrow or next year. The border between what was and what will be is called NOW. *Now is where we live life – or miss life.*

For our purpose there are **three major seasons** of life: the first childhood, the interim and the second childhood. The phrase 'second childhood' usually is used in a derogatory way. But biblical wisdom honors elders because they have worked through the complexities of life and have come to realize they do not know much. They are willing to listen to others and to God. They have become like little children. They are open to hear from God and others because they do not think they already know (*that is if they are elders and not merely old*).

Retiring from the college campus in 2004 was for me another leaving home for the pilgrim's journey. I had to learn who I am without students challenging or hanging on my words in a classroom.

The term I use for these transitional periods (the time between the times) is limen. A limen is experienced as "no longer but not yet." Some transformations happen quickly like crossing the city limit (limen) or a state line. We move quickly from being in Oklahoma to being in Texas even though things do not look any different. Few transitions in life are that simple or that fast. The border between countries is a better example. A border is an area where you are no longer in the US but not yet in Mexico for example. We remain in the border-space (limen) until we process through the requirements of customs and the duty station.

At any given point in life we are no longer what we were and not yet what we will be. We find another useful example in architecture. In many public buildings, like arenas, theaters and churches, there is an area called the foyer or the vestibule. You are no longer outside but you are not yet in the sanctuary, arena or theater proper.

It is called a vestibule because in that space we divest ourselves of the things that were proper outside (the past) and put on the vestments proper for the inside (the future). Our lives are actually lived in the vestibule we call NOW. We are always moving away from what we were yesterday and forward into what we will be tomorrow. *To stop moving is to stop living.*

The final transition is death. Some have had what we call near death experiences and have reported something of the new reality on the "other side" of this time-space reality. In my opinion most of them were only in the vestibule of eternity. What they often report is a tunnel or a meadow on the way into the other side of reality. So there may be transitions there as well.

We began this book with the question, "Who am I really?" At this stage in my life I realize the answer to this question is simple. I no longer identify myself by words important others have spoken over me. My past failures *or* accomplishments do not define me. I do not identify myself by any position I have achieved or role I have played in life. I am identified with Jesus Christ in His death, burial and resurrection. I saw this truth logically years ago but I still inwardly identified myself as a PhD or as a teacher in the Body of Christ. Still later I identified with Jesus as a son; his Father is also my Father.

We now raise the question differently: "Who am I before I speak? Who am I between my words? Who am I after I speak? Between my thoughts? Before I do?"

186

As I raise this question another more significant question presents itself: *"What was I 'sent here' to do?"* In other words, an issue more basic than who I am is what I was designed to do; what is in the acorn? Many spend their time trying to find their true identity and fail to discover their true **destiny**.

The most recent step into perceiving who I really am will require some background. Stay with me because this could be a bumpy ride for some.

I Am that I Am

When Moses asked God for His name God simply said, "I AM that I AM." The Jewish people considered this name so holy that they refused to pronounce it except in certain rituals that required the priest to pronounce it. While reading the text they replace the NAME with the word "Lord." When the early Church called Jesus Lord they were identifying Him with the God who made His presence known to Moses at the burning bush. Jesus "is the image [what you actually see] of the invisible God," Paul said (Colossians 1:15).

This name comes into English transliteration as YHWH (without vowels) or YaHWeH (with vowels).

Paul said of himself, *"I am what I am by the grace of God"* (II Corinthians 15:10). Paul also referred to himself in several other ways. He was "…as to the Law, blameless," he was an apostle, a bondservant and he was a spiritual father. All those are accomplishments, positions, roles and functions. When he said, "I am what I am," he was not referring to any of those. He was not enamored with his position, his function or his

187

accomplishments. He was willing to accept himself as one who would be nothing apart from the grace of God.

Standing Beside Yourself

Paul was known as Saul of Tarsus before he became an apostle. He took himself seriously before the Light put him on the ground (Acts. 9:1-9). He was self-confident, intense and possessed with a purpose: to destroy the new sect rising out of the ministry of Jesus of Nazareth. He was a proud man *standing tall within himself.* We might suspect that his father encouraged him to believe in himself. He may have received a T-shirt that read, "Mighty-Man-of-God."

He had studied under Gamaliel II, one of the seven greatest Rabbis in the history of Israel. Gamaliel II only accepted top level students with the highest potential as disciples. Saul excelled beyond all his peers and probably would have become one of the great Rabbis of Judaism had it not been for that Light that knocked the props out from under his proud stance. His new journey began on the ground with blindness having to be led by others.

Very little is known about the next fourteen years of his life. We do know that he did not lose his intensity. Because of that intensity the disciples in Jerusalem had to send him away so there would be peace (Acts. 9:30-31). We also know that he spent three years in Arabia. Some think he was trying to work through his own "*Who Am I really?*" questions. I think it is more likely he was seeking an answer to the question he raised when the light struck him down: "*What would you have me to do?*" Then he spent several years in his home town of Tarsus before

188

Barnabas found him and made him part of a leadership group in Antioch. His new journey shifted to missions for the One he had persecuted.

His personal intensity continued to manifest itself with the new vision: to win the world to Christ. His natural gifts as a man, his basic nature, had not changed but his way of identifying himself went through several changes as he seized life experiences as opportunities to be changed into the likeness of the One he met on the Damascus Road. He understood Christ-likeness as an image reflected in one's lifestyle of willingness to empty himself of his ego for the sake of others. *Paul was learning how to love as he was loved.*

This commitment to lay down his self-life for others brought him into many trials. His difficulty with false apostles and false brothers was probably more painful than the lashings, stonings and beatings he received (II Corinthians 11). He understood that the treasure in him, the Christ in him, could only be made available through the cracking of the vessel (II Corinthians 4:7-12). He was willing to die to himself daily so life might come through him to others. Love is willing to suffer for others.

He was no longer standing tall within himself. "It is no longer I who live," he wrote, "but Christ who lives in me. And the life I now live in the flesh I live by faith of the Son of God, who loved me and gave himself for me" (Galatians 2:20). In this text there is the "I" that is "no longer I" and there is the "I" that is Christ in him living the Christ-life through him. Paul was no longer taking himself seriously. His heart was no longer lifted up and his eyes were not raised too high.

Paul was standing beside his True Self – the Christ

in him. The Christ was living out his love-life through Paul. Jesus came to make the Father known as the God who is Love. He made Father known by living a life of loving God and his neighbor. Jesus demonstrated Father's love by laying down his life for the world His Father created. Paul made Jesus known in the same way. In First Corinthians 13 Paul said that love does not boast. Love does not take itself or its accomplishments seriously. Love simply does the right thing without boasting.

We see this in Paul's defense against false apostles. He did not boast of his spirituality or his accomplishments as many do. He boasted of his weaknesses. When he did mention his spiritual experiences he wrote, "I know a man in Christ who fourteen years ago was caught up to the third heaven . . . and he heard things that cannot be told, which man may not utter. On behalf of this man I will boast" (II Corinthians 12:2-5). Many scholars agree he was speaking of himself as though he spoke of another man. That posture is what I have in mind when I say Paul was *standing beside himself*. He pointed to his spiritual experience as though he were speaking of another man.

My Story Abridged

I received with meekness my dad's word that I was dumb. I experienced shame because of that false identity so I donned several cover-ups to hide what I considered to be my true self – the Dumb-Dumb. First it was a Clown Suit, then a Smart-Suit, a Double-Smart suit with a long overcoat, and finally a Super-Smart metal armor. None of those were effective in ridding me of the shame. I still felt dumb. My journey into freedom took me through several experiences of taking off the outfits I had slipped into. I no longer need the academic certificates or the accolades.

When I finally realized that Father God had gifted me with academic and analytical abilities I became proud. When I recognized my pride I began to hide my credentials so people would not think I was proud (which means I was proud but unwilling to face it). In my attempt to take off the cover-ups which I had donned I was trying to "crucify the old man." I refused to acknowledge my education. I was afraid people would think I was boastful. *But I was actually crucifying the new man in Christ*. It was actually a false humility. False humility is another form of pride.

Others apparently recognized my teaching gift. Several times after delivering a message I have had people refer to me as "America's best kept secret" as a Bible teacher. I heard that comment first in 1976 and I continue to hear it today. That statement recognizes the fact that I am not very well known; it is like I have been in the shadows rather than in the limelight. It is true that I have never been free to openly promote myself for fear of being perceived as proud. There I go again with false humility.

As I moved toward a higher level of maturity it dawned on me that I had identified myself with my teaching gift. I know I am a gifted teacher but the gift is not me; it is something *given* to me. I still wanted to prove myself worthy of the gifted-teacher role by correcting other people's doctrines. I had to prove my point often at the expense of the feelings of the student asking the question or suggesting another interpretation. *I was standing tall within myself as a gifted teacher.* I was being rude. Love is not rude (I Corinthians 13).

Wrestling with this new insight I came to see myself as simply *a son of God who is allowed to teach*. This looks much humbler; but even here there is a hidden pride, hidden especially from me. My identity was in being a *privileged son* who did not need to prove himself worthy of the position of teacher. But I still found myself trying to prove how humble I was. Occasionally I would slip up and correct someone's doctrine anyway. I was still falling short of loving as He loves.

I was reading John 15:15 where Jesus said, "No longer do I call you servants, for the servant does not know what his master is doing; but I have called you friends, for all that I have heard from my Father I have made known to you." He is a Son who is friends with His Father. Then I saw this: *I am a son, but I am also a friend who has access to the Father's plan*. He shows me what He is doing. Then I remembered that I experienced Jesus as my friend when I was a boy. But I began to use this as a badge of honor. "I am a friend of God." I was still standing tall within myself as a friend of God.

We Need a Helper

The next spiritual growth spurt came when I realized that the above identities are *all* based on position, relationship, performance or gift. Son refers to a position, friend speaks of a relationship and the gift is not who I am. I am not the "coat of many colors;" I wear it. *So who is the "I" that is me inside this coat my Father gave me?*

With Paul I simply say, "I am what I am by the grace of God," or more simply, "**I am what I am**." This identity statement can be declared even more simply, "**I am**." The real question is whether I am able to stay in this simple identity or will I try to prove to others that I am something in particular, something that will impress them. I still struggle with that regularly.

Flashes of insight often come to me as I study. I am often content to process the insights with my head and develop logical descriptions of what I saw. Getting the insights worked into my life is an ongoing process. In our culture we tend to think it is enough to understand with our mind. That is our culture's way of dealing with life, and that is what I often do. We may even try to behave in the way we think is proper in light of the insight but it seldom works out as we think it should. *We all need a helper in this matter of living out of what we know.*

Our Creator knows we need help; He created us to need help because He wants us to lean on Him as our helper. The help He wants to offer is not of the codependent kind. He wants to be with us and do things together with us. He wants to be part of our lives. He wants intimacy. This helper is closer to us than a brother or friend. Actually the fact that this helper is so close keeps us from receiving His help. How close is He?

Our Helper is Inside

Paul reminded the Corinthians that "he who is joined to the Lord becomes one spirit with him" (I Corinthians 6:17). Theologians have given very little attention to this truth partly because we have thought of the soul and spirit as the same thing. We all have a human spirit by virtue of the divine breath breathed into the human race. When one is joined to the Lord, when the word-seed is united to the ovum of the human spirit, it is "wed" to the Holy Spirit. That means we who are begotten of God have 24/7 access to the Trinitarian God through our human spirit.

One difficulty is that our spirit is not always part of our conscious awareness. We sometimes expect the Holy Spirit to speak to us from "out there." We are trained by our culture to be aware of what is out there rather than what is inside us. Our focus is on externals. We notice what others are doing but seldom see ourselves as a part of the mix. We react to the "triggers" before we get in touch with the spirit within who knows God's heart.

Let me give an example. A lady came to me complaining that her third husband was responding to her the same way the first two had responded. She wanted advice on how to change her husband. I asked her what all three of these relationships had in common. (It was a trick question.) She began to speak of the things each man had done wrong and how they had belittled her and made her feel horrible. It was clear to me that she triggered her husbands and her husbands triggered her. But she had only seen what her husbands were doing. She had not looked within herself.

After she had almost run out of offenses to mention I said, "There is one more thing all those experiences have in common." She asked me what I meant. I continued, "You were there; you were the wife." At first she was shocked. Then she realized she was part of the problem. She had actually triggered her husbands' reactions. She realized her attitude had invited the abuse. She understood how much she needed a helper. She had not seen the good in her husbands because she had not yet seen good in herself as one whom God loves. Christ was in her but unable to express His love through her.

The point here is that we are tuned to what is happening outside of us rather than noticing the still small voice of the One *inside* us, the One who wants to be our friend and helper. *It is difficult to recognize His help because He is inside while we are looking outside.* He is a part of who we are because we are one spirit with Him. He abides in us and we abide in Him. St. Augustine in his *Confessions* noticed that God cannot be found in the world until He is first found in our heart. Once we find Him within ourselves we will begin to see His image in other human beings around us.

Our helper is not pushy. He does not try to control our lives to make us do the right thing. God is Love. Love does not insist on its own way (I Corinthians 13:5). God will allow us to go our own way until we realize we need His help. He is not after right behavior; He is after our heart. He wants to be with us as the Helper who is inside, who is closer than a brother. But He is not content to merely *be* inside. He wants to live his love-life through us. Paul Billheimer made this point in his book, *Don't Waste Your Sorrows*. He noted that, if at the end of our life we have learned to love, we will have learned what we were put here to learn. I would state it this way, *"We will have learned to do what we were sent here to do."*

Striving to Enter Rest

None of us will come to genuine rest until we find that place in Father's house which Jesus went to prepare for us (John 14:2). It is enlightening to notice this text

195

does not mention heaven. The text is not talking about going to heaven. Jesus went to prepare a place within the *house* of God – a place to function within His Temple which is the Body of Christ in the earth. That place in Father's house is secured for us but we must enter by the narrow gate. To get through this narrow vestibule we must lay down our baggage and slip into the kingdom vestments. To enter the kingdom of God we must leave our own personal kingdom behind.

Another way of speaking of the place He prepared for us is the place of Sabbath rest. Jesus was at rest when He worked miracles on the Sabbath because His Father was the One who was doing the work through Him (John 14:10). He lived his life on earth in his Father's house doing His will. He prepared a place for us in that house and invites us to join Him in that place of rest. His goal is to accomplish Father's work in us and through us as we come to rest in Him and allow Father to do His work.

In the book of Hebrews this Sabbath rest is available to the people of God. It is clear from that context that the *rest is related to **hearing the voice** of God*. "Today, if you hear his voice, do not harden your hearts as in the rebellion" (Hebrews 3:7, 8, 15 and 4:7). The place of rest is where we are listening for the still small voice which offers help through the living and abiding Word of God. The text continues, "Let us therefore strive to enter that rest, so that no one may fall by the same sort of disobedience," (4:11-12).

We have unconscious programing that responds to triggers rather than listening for the voice. It takes effort to go against what we learned growing up and receiving an education (even if that education was in the school of hard knocks). We must *strive* to leave the old ways. Paul was talking about this when he said we must crucify the old man so the new man can come alive in Christ. It is all about learning to love others as Father loves us. This is a paradox. *We must **strive** to enter into this **rest**.*

I was sharing a word with a friend about the Holy Spirit. He was raised in the same legalistic tradition as I was. His response surprised me, "If I agree with what you are saying I would have to admit I have been wrong all these years." I honestly do not think he heard what he was saying. He would rather stay with a lie than admit he had been wrong. He was striving against Father's love that was being offered. The ovum of his spirit was resisting the word-seed. Later he began to listen for the voice; the seed had penetrated the ovum. He allowed his "old man" to die and slipped into the vestments of his "new man."

Is God at Rest?

Some might be shocked by that question. Most of our time and effort is spent trying to come to rest in God. There is a series of fifteen psalms that describe the pilgrim's journey (Psalms 120-134). The first twelve of these psalms focus on the struggles of the pilgrim to find a place of rest in the lap of God. In Psalm 131 David found a place of rest as a child held by his mother. Our tendency is to think this is the final destination. We think we will have arrived when we get to that place of rest.

But in Psalm 132 there is a major shift in the paradigm. David began to concern himself with finding a resting place for God. He committed himself to experience no personal rest until he found a dwelling

197

place for the Mighty One of Jacob. When we read this through New Testament eyes we realize that *the resting place which God is looking for is within us*. We are the temple (house) of God and His Holy Spirit dwells within us (I Corinthians 3:16). God wants to *come to rest in us*.

I like to speak of it in this way: I invited Jesus to come in and offered Him a seat in the easy chair. He said, "I did not come to visit; I came to take over. Show me your kitchen (eating habits)." I tried to clean it up but He had to help me. He then wanted to see my bedroom (sexual fantasies). I tried again but He had to help me with that as well. I needed even more help with my bank account (spending habits) and time management. He is not yet totally at rest in me. Is He at rest in you? Or does he still have work to do?

The Great I AM wants to come to rest in me as I come to rest in the Great I AM. He comes to rest in me when I am willing to simply BE-in-Him. We strive against this because we do not realize that coming to rest in Him is coming to rest in Love. "I am what I am by the grace of God" means *I am in Him as He loves me, and He is in me as I love others*. I no longer need to say I am this or I am that. **I am simply who I am by allowing Him to be who He is in and through me**. It is not about what I do or don't do, or what I say or don't say. It is about receiving His love and passing it on to others.

Today I am simply going to be me, "me-at-rest-in-Him," as I do whatever He shows me He is doing. The issue is not what I *should* do today, it is all about simply being in Him and doing today what he is leading me to do at this time and in this place which is called "*here and now*." We live and breathe in this limen, in this vestibule.

When we do what He is doing, we are being who we are in Him and doing what we were sent here to do.

Obedience to the Truth

The springboard for the final step of our journey together will be a statement Peter made in the context of being begotten of the word of God. "Having purified your souls by your obedience to the truth for a sincere love of the brethren," he wrote, "love one another earnestly from the heart" (I Peter 1:22). The goal of purifying the soul is to be able to love as God loves. Like St. John of the Cross, we believe that the goal of life here on earth is to learn how to love as He loves. Since God is love it follows that we are "wired for love" as Dr. Caroline Leaf says.

The purifying of the soul is related to the process we earlier called the salvation (or *sozo* healing) of the soul. We have difficulty loving sincerely before our helper heals our behavior mechanism – our soul.

The love of the brethren will only be a cover for our self-seeking as long as our soul is not purified; we want our brothers and sisters to like us, or we want them to do something for us. Jack Frost, founder of Shiloh Place, called it "love with a hook in it." We pretend to love because we want something. Pure love is cleansed from all ulterior motives. Pure love can only come from a purified soul. Otherwise we cover our true motives lest others find out what we really want from the relationship. (One problem is that we are seldom aware that we are covering something; we believe our own pretense.)

Our interest here is the phrase "obedience to the truth." Both words in this phrase need attention. Normally

199

we think of a system of rules regulating behavior when we see the word *obedience*. "Do this and don't do that," we think. And we do not normally think of *truth* as something to obey. We think truth is something to believe. A quick word study will help solve this difficulty.

The word truth (*alethea*) is a negated form of a word referring to a *veil that covers what is there*. In its negated form it refers to something that is being uncovered or unveiled. With the veil removed we see what is really there; we see truth or reality. Man can uncover many things but the truth of God can only be uncovered by God himself. We call it *revelation*. "Flesh and blood has not revealed this to you," Jesus said to Peter, "but my Father who is in heaven" (Matthew 16:16). In this sense ***truth is an event*** *in which reality is uncovered* for the individual or for the group. They see it; they get it in their heart.

The word Peter used for obedience in this text is *hupakoe*, "to hear under." To obey in this sense means to place yourself in submission under the word you hear from the one who is speaking. The word submission actually means to place yourself under (sub) the mission of another. Submission is hearkening to the voice. **Biblical faith is a submissive response to the presence of the speaking God**. Faithfulness is a life lived in the presence of the speaking God in meekness and humility. There are several categories of truth to obey.

We will discuss three categories: 1) commissions, 2) promises and 3) affirmations. **Commissions** are the commands of God to bring man into alignment with Himself and His kingdom. There is ***something to do*** in response to what is ***unveiled*** as His will. **Promises** are the ultimate realities offered to those who believe. There is

200

something to receive in response to what is *unveiled* as available to us. **Affirmations** are words spoken to the heart of the believers to strengthen and encourage them in who they are in Christ. There is *something to accept about yourself* in response to His opening your eyes to see who you really are. In each case something is unveiled for those who have eyes to see and ears to hear.

We will use Jesus as an example of obedience to a *commission*. Jesus healed on the Sabbath (John 5) because He was doing what he saw His Father doing. If He had been responding to a law code He would have done nothing because of the Sabbath laws. If He had been responding to a legal notion of His call to heal, He would have tried to heal the multitude at the pool. He saw His Father healing one man and understood it as a *commission to heal that one*. He *heard under* that commission, healed that one man and waited for further instructions.

When we hearken to the voice of Father we are *purged of the self-will* that moves us out of the flow of abundant life. *This is the obedience of FAITH.*

The story of Abram illustrates an obedient response to a *promise*. God promised a son to Abram. His obedience to this promise was that "he believed the Lord and it was counted to him as righteousness" (Genesis 15:6). Notice it says he believed the Lord, not the promise. He obviously believed the promise and expected a son; but primarily he believed God. Abram *heard under* the word he received in the presence of the speaking God. That faith did not make him perfect. Later he *heard under* the voice of his wife and produced Ishmael (Genesis

201

16:2). Even with that he did not cease to hope for the son of promise.

When we hearken to the voice of Father telling us what He is offering us we are *purged of the false hopes* that create inordinate passions. *This is the obedience of HOPE.* This obedience brings us to have true biblical hope. Abram hoped against hope because of his faith.

Now we come to truth in the form of **affirmation**. This book has been about this form of truth from the beginning. Most of our unrest comes from *hearing under* false words about who we are and what we are destined to be and to do. We may hear those false words from important others or we may speak those words to ourselves. The words we have received with meekness determine the successes and failures of life.

When we hearken to the affirming voice of Father we are *purged of the feelings of abandonment and rejection* which cause us to feel all alone. *This is the obedience of LOVE.* This obedience allows us to experience the love of Father and prods us to love others as we are loved.

I AM ... At Rest

The "Great I AM" and my "little I am" are one; He is in me and I am in Him. This is not a numerical one; it is a relational one. It is the one of union. I am not Him and He is not me anymore than I am my wife and my wife is me. We are married and we are one in the sense of the union of intimate fellowship. *My union with God does not make me a god; it simply connects me to Him as my source, my security and my destiny.* If I want to find God I must look within the secret place of my heart; that is where He lives. That is where He is (Matthew 6:5-6). And from that place in me He wants to love others.

I am at rest in my present level of development. "What we will be has not yet appeared," John wrote, "but we know that when he appears we shall be like him, because we will see him as he is," (I John 3:2). I am not yet what I will be in him, but I am no longer what I was without him. I am a human becoming fully human by slipping into the vestments of love. Paul had the same thing in mind when he wrote, "When Christ who is our life is revealed, then you also will be revealed with him in glory" (Colossians 3:4).

His glory is His love shinning forth through those who *hear under* His still small voice. He will tell us how to love if we will listen. St. Irenaeus, one of the early Church Fathers, saw the glory of God as a human being who was fully alive. We simply need to be fully alive in Him allowing Him to love through us. In that way, and only in that way, we glorify God. He is not glorified by our fleshly attempts to make Him look good.

I am at rest in the process of striving to become a fully alive human by loving as Father loves. I am working out my *sozo* healing with fear and trembling. *Father is at rest in me as He works in me* "both to will and to work according to his good pleasure" (Philippians 2:12-13). This is one of the many paradoxes of the Christian life: He does all the work as we strive to enter His love-rest.

This brings to our attention a further insight. *God never changes but He does move.* Jesus "is, was and is to come" (Revelation 1:8). Notice the "is" is before the "was." He IS (before He was) and He has a past and a future. He is no longer in the flesh on earth (His past) but He is already seated at the right hand of the Father (Now). He is presently in the world with you and with me, but He has not yet brought all His enemies under his feet (His future). His enemies are not people but the powers that alienate people from one another and from Him. So I find my identity in Him but I am not yet what I will be. I am a human becoming one who allows the divine love to flow through me to bring freedom to others. I am coming to rest in love. I am on the way as a pilgrim.

This introduces a final insight: *there is no "I" that is finished and alone.* We are all connected to one another and we are all on our way to wholeness. We are all in relationship with others. God's image in us is relational because God is love and love is relational. As a fellow human we are in relationship with every other human. That relationship may be good, bad or distant. We are still related as humans. We are related (in different ways) to those who receive us and to those who reject us. There is no such thing as love without a relationship with another. That is why we are called to love even our enemies.

Now I simply say, "I am with you as I am with Him. Together we are on our way to *sozo* healing, on our way to the wholeness of being fully human, manifesting the divine nature of love in our community." We are each at different points on this journey. (This includes prodigals and those Graham Cooke calls "pre-Christian.")

Jesus said what we do to others we also do to him. When I receive a fellow human I receive Him. If I shut down to a fellow human I also shut down to Jesus because

God created every human in His image. Even if this person has not yet received the word-seed he is already called to receive it. The image of God in every human is like an ovum, as we have said. If it has not received the seed it can never grow into His likeness, but that image is there in every human.

If the ovum has received the word-seed the person is begotten of God and needs to receive word-milk and continual *sozo* healing. So a person does not receive the image of God when he is born again because every human is created in the image of God. *But when one is begotten of God he receives the* **potential** *of growing into His likeness* from one degree of glory to another.

My heart has been transformed by this realization: I experience oneness with Him as I open myself to you, a fellow human. (Remember, what we do to others we do to Him.) We are connected as humans. And humanity is connected to Him as Creator. This connection does not imply agreement nor does it imply a common destiny. *The* **destiny** *of being conformed to His image becomes a reality for us as we* **receive the seed in which that destiny resides**. Without that seed we can only live our lives as humans trying (or not trying) to become something we are **not yet** capable of becoming. The word-seed must be received before transformation is possible.

I am at rest striving to enter rest in Father's bosom. In His bosom is love for the whole world and that includes those who are pre-Christian. So without you I cannot be the one I am in Him any more than I can be the one I am without Him. Life is a journey of striving to enter into this love-rest. All fear and anxiety is vanquished by the light of His face when this insight dawns on us. As this light

205

dawns I can begin to see His face in people I formally rejected. I can see His goodness in those who reject me.

The focus is not tied to the question, "Who am I?" Life is not about discovering who I am; that is necessary but it is not the point. *Life is something you do*. But the doing is not driven by a desire to be recognized, to be appreciated or to prove something. Life is about reflecting the glory of our Creator by loving others as He has loved us. The basic question of life is addressed to the Source of all life: "*What would you have me do today?*"

So I conclude this part of my journey and return to living life, discovering what it means that I am at rest in Him and in relationship with you, doing today what He calls me to do today. I am a baby word learning how to be a clear expression of the divine nature of love. This is what we are created for. *This is what we are called, sent and empowered to do.*

In and of myself I can do nothing of lasting value, but I am not in and of myself. I am in Him and I am of Him. I am not alone with myself and God; I am at rest in Father's bosom while I am with you. As He comes to rest in me I go with you to rest in His Love. I am in Love and at rest with you as a partner if you choose to join me in the journey of becoming fully human in Him together.

I have returned to the age of simply being.

Join me in this journey together with Christ – from the bosom of the Father into the bosom of the Father.

206

ENDORSEMENTS

It is an immeasurable gift for someone to discover who they are and what they're here to do. Fount has given a great gift in presenting a clear path that aids in that discovery. The generations need to gain courage and direction from what's offered here and to rise together on their way to genuine intimate relationships.

Eric Reeder, Founder of RISE movement
www.generationsrise.com

Many of us go through life perplexed by the twists and turns of the journey and never figure out what is going on. We often feel like life is uncertain and unexplainable. Fount writes, "The basic desire of fatherhood, as such, is to see His own image and likeness reproduced in His sons. It is also true, that the reality of sonship, as such, is seen in the capacity to grow into the likeness of the Father." You will find this book immensely valuable in understanding what the Father is developing in you and how you are growing into His likeness through this journey in Christ, called life.

Robert Muncy
Apostolic Leader, The House of Praise for All People
Greenwood, DE www.houseevents.us

Fount takes us on this journey by creatively illustrating how the words spoken over us have influenced our direction in life. He shows the way out of the old into the new. He is so transparent and intimate that you find yourself in the story line. Hang on, because the answers you have been desperately seeking are uncovered through the experiences and life stages of this little boy trying to become the man Father created him to be.

Great read for those who are truly seeking to be the person you know you were supposed to become.

Trisha Frost
Co-Founder of Shiloh Place Ministries
https://shilohplace.org

65379863R00126

Made in the USA
Middletown, DE
02 September 2019